Hospitality Sales and Marketing

HOSPIALITY SALES AND MARKETING

D.K. SINGH

Vice-President

Heritage Institute of Hotel and Tourism

Agra

AMAN PUBLICATIONS

NEW DELHI

Published by
Rajiv Jain for Aman Publications
LG-4A, Ganpati Bhawan,
4675-B/21, Ansari Road,
Darya Ganj, Delhi - 110002
PH: 23255012, 23282127
E-mail: sshjbs@yahoo.com

First Published – 2010

ISBN–81–8204–048-052-3
ISBN–978-81–8204--052-6

SOLE DISTRIBUTOR
JINDAL BOOK SERVICES
LG-4A, Ganpati Bhawan,
4675-B/21, Ansari Road,
Darya Ganj, Delhi - 110002

Jacket Designed by :
S.M. Graphics

Printed by:
NCT Printers & Publishers, Delhi, India

Preface

You will be able to customise and personalise your marketing and sales communications according to your members' activities and measure your results in real time. 'Hospitality Sales and marketing' is the essential guide for every manager in the hospitality industry wanting to achieve maximum profits from their sales promotions.

Staying in touch is made easier - and more profitable - with Customer Relationship Management programme (CRM). CRM is a simple to use, yet robust and agile web-based application that links member usage and customer data directly with reporting systems and campaign management tools. CRM enables HMC's partner hotels to manage their loyalty programme, member databases, marketing initiatives, member recognition, as well as monitor programme performance.

Practical and down-to-earth, this book covers:

- Introduction to Hospitality Sales and Marketing
- Hotel Marketing and Sales
- Destination Marketing Strategy
- Hospitality Business Promotion
- Quality Service Marketing
- Technology in Hospitality Marketing
- New Realities of Hospitality Sales
- Challenges of Revenue Management
- Hospitality Partnerships 265

This book provides in-depth instruction based on the strategies of leading hospitality organisations. It introduces crucial sales and marketing concepts and describes how they apply to hospitality businesses and customers. It familiarise students in any undergraduate programme to the real world of hospitality sales and gives them the solid grounding they will need to embark on a successful career in hospitality sales.

Combining marketing theory with a strong practical emphasis on industry applications, this offers superior coverage of marketing as an integral part of operations, especially at the unit level. It guides readers through the basics of marketing research, segmentation, and targeting, as well as branding, distribution, location, pricing, and communication. It gives future hospitality professionals an important career-building resource for virtually every area of the field.

An essential, practical and explanatory guide to sales promotion and marketing.

D.K. SINGH

Contents

1

Introduction to Hospitality Sales and Marketing

Marketing is an on-going, patron-driven process that requires determining patron needs and desires and then delivering programs and/or services to meet those needs and desires.

Basic Functions of Marketing

To provide your patrons with the product or program they desire, you must consider the marketing mix, or the four "P's" which are the basic functions of marketing-product, price, place, and promotion.

Product

A product may be defined as a thing produced by an action, operation, or labor; a result. A product should include a set of intangible, psychological attributes as well as the tangible end product. Some examples of intangible attributes are convenience, taste, and satisfaction to the customer. Your goal should be to offer the product that gives your customers their desired product attributes and level of quality.

Price

Price is the value assigned to something bought, sold, or offered for sale. The value must include the way a market responds to price. To determine the best price, you can rely on one or both of these two methods: cost-plus and/ or demand-oriented. The cost-plus method requires a knowledge of various types of costs: fixed costs, variable costs, and total costs. The demand-oriented method requires knowledge of this data and knowledge of what your market is willing to pay for your product. You assign the price at which your customers will purchase your product.

Place

Place, in marketing terms, encompasses distribution channels and the method used to distribute your product. You must distribute (sell) your product in the areas where there is demand for it. Your product should also be available when it is desired. An example of "place" is distributing hamburgers in a restaurant and not in a department store.

Promotion

You can conduct a great market analysis, develop the best product, and set the right price; but if customers are not aware of your product, all your efforts are in vain. Promotion is the process of informing customers of availability and convincing them to buy. To state this more simply-promotion is telling and selling.

Marketing Process

The marketing process provides management with specific information about the patron and non-patron. It is the information that allows management to target specific groups towards specific programs. The marketing process provides the data for planning program objectives; i.e., hours of operation, number of employees, types of equipment needed, patron likes and dislikes, etc. Above all, by using marketing principles, management can promote the benefits of patronising the activity. When the patron needs correlate with benefits and the perceived value of participation, the potential for increased usage exists.

Marketing Research

Managers can no longer just open the doors to a facility and expect patrons to flock in. Market research will help identify your patron's needs and desires. Research methods include questionnaires, formal surveys, participant comment cards, focus groups, and informal observation. Once the decision is made to conduct research, the first step is to determine exactly what type of information is needed.

Research Methods

There are numerous methods available to management for conducting marketing research. Some of the methods are ongoing processes while others are for a specific length of time. The more familiar techniques include:

— *Asking:* Patrons and potential patrons should routinely be asked about their likes, dislikes, desires, and needs concerning the food and hospitality program. MWR personnel should seek information form both users and non-users. Many civilian-sector restaurants, clubs, and hotels make calls to their patrons to find out their feelings about services offered.

— *Observing:* The employees and activity manager should observe patrons. Observation can provide many clues about levels of satisfaction and usage.

— Suggestion Boxes: The suggestion box is a useful and effective management tool if used correctly. The boxes should be located in high traffic areas, must be well maintained, and have paper and pencils available. To further elicit patron participation, patron comments should be acted upon and the action publicised.

— *After-Action Reports:* Evaluating after-action reports received from activity and program managers can be helpful for planning future activities. By preparing in-depth reports, mistakes can be avoided and new personnel will not have to reinvent the wheel each time a program is offered. Historically, after-action reports have helped in assessing trends and predicting future programming needs.

— *Questionnaires:* There are two types of questionnaires, informal and formal, that can elicit vital information from patrons.

— *Informal Questionnaires:* These surveys can be accomplished on the spot (intercept interviews) and do not utilise the scientific method. Informal questionnaires should be kept as short as possible and are meant to be given to patrons while they are participating in an activity or shortly thereafter. They should not cause the patron any inconvenience.

Although an informal questionnaire does not provide scientific data, it does provide information about the patron's attitude towards the program. Furthermore, if this survey is accomplished "on the spot" the information gained from the patron is timely and accurate because the experience is still vivid in the patron's mind. Specific trends are also easily noted if the information is analysed immediately.

Promotion Strategies

Promotion is the process of communicating between your activity and your eligible patrons, the media, other agencies, your command, your management, and staff. Promotion consists of informing, persuading, and influencing the patron. It increases awareness and understanding and allows patrons to become more knowledgeable and thus more discriminating. Through promotion, you can inform patrons of the benefits your activity offers, and how your activity is distinctively different from other similar establishments.

To make promotion decisions, you should cover at least four areas:

(1) define the product characteristics

(2) establish promotion objectives

(3) determine the nature of the message, including timing and frequency

(4) determine the promotion-mix patterns which will effectively and efficiently deliver the message. By systematically approaching this decision process, your chances to maximise success will be increased.

Food and hospitality and marketing managers, working together, can develop the most successful promotion and communication program. A number of promotional methods should be used, and to be effective, promotions must be constantly repeated. In the commercial sector, a message is repeated at least six times before the individual is motivated to either visit a hotel or go to a restaurant.

Types of promotional tools

There are many ways to promote your program. Try to vary the types of promotional tools you use for different events or activities. Some of the promotional tools you have at your disposal include:

Advertising

Advertising is a method of communicating with consumers, and is used to stimulate repeat business, introduce new services, and announce any changes in regular services and/or facilities. It is usually accomplished through newspapers, magazines, brochures, flyers, radio, and television. The primary objective of advertising is to keep patrons aware of club services and programs. It is especially important that advertising be used frequently since there are many potential patrons arriving on the base daily and for short periods of duty. Food and hospitality activities cannot rely on their past reputation because of this high turnover.

The second objective of advertising is to provide a favorable image of club offerings. This may also be referred to as the "soft sell" approach. The objective is not to sell specific services or programs through advertising, but rather to sell by advertising the activity itself. For example, the Temporary Lodging Facility (TLF) might distribute a brochure stating the facility's location, along with some simple remark such as: "If you are expecting out-of-town guests, think of us." No specific products or services are mentioned; it is merely a notice of the TLF's availability.

The third objective is often referred to as "pre-sell." This occurs when there are specific promotions, specials, or benefits that are to be communicated. The "pre-sell" objective is applied to advertising which is aimed at inducing immediate action. A special limited time offer and special one-night entertainment are examples of this approach.

It is important to remember these objectives before implementing an advertising program. Each program will have its particular requirements and, in order to be effective, should be specific in nature according to its purpose.

There are two strategies in advertising, direct and indirect.

— *Direct advertising* is when the patron is encouraged to immediately take advantage of a service. For example, if food and hospitality has a promotion scheduled for a limited time, direct advertisements should stress that the timeliness of the promotion is critical. Direct advertising is intense over a limited period of time.

— *Indirect advertising,* however, attempts to create a long-range demand for the service. This method instills in patrons the knowledge that a service or program is available if and when they are interested in pursuing it. For example, if the Enlisted Club has Happy Hour every Friday throughout the year, or offers check cashing, indirect advertising is the method that should be used to promote this particular offering.

Public Relations

Public relations (PR) refers to the total image projected by an organisation. Efforts that establish, maintain, and improve activity image are all part of PR, and consist of advertising, packaging, customer relations, and corporate policy. For food and hospitality, PR involves the creation of a positive patron attitude and goodwill toward the activity. The day-to-day image conveyed through employees, management practices, and the physical facility is more important than any other advertising and is essential to success. An activity's perceived image can attract or turn away potential patrons.

Sales Promotion

This technique is designed to stimulate patron involvement in programs food and hospitality activities wish to promote.

There are at least four types of sales promotion. They are:

— *Sampling:* This is an attempt to pre-sell the activity and/or service to the patron. For example, the base restaurant may want to promote a new dessert menu by providing an opportunity for patrons to sample a small piece of the "dessert of the evening", free of charge. This gives patrons a chance to sample the food with the idea that they will like it and be influenced to purchase it, or another dessert, the next time they dine at the restaurant.

— *Coupons:* Coupons are used by 70 percent of American retailers in promoting products. Some commands provide MWR coupons good for reduced charges at MWR activities to stimulate interest and participation. Couponing has yet to reach its full impact. A coupon gives the patron the opportunity to participate in an activity at reduced or no cost. They can be very effective with new personnel assigned to the command, used as a motivational tool for them to visit your activity.

— *Contests:* A contest may be used as a promotional method directed toward creating additional enthusiasm and interest. Contests usually provide some form of prizes. An example of a contest to promote enthusiasm and interest in a particular activity is a chili cook-off, held at the snackbar, judged by your staff, and a featured menu for a period of time, in hopes that the contest will encourage patrons to visit the snackbar more often.

— *Demonstrations:* To create interest in your menu specialties or new Chef, a cooking demonstration might be arranged to take place at the exchange mall or at a booth during an MWR festival.

Personal Selling

Perhaps the most under-utilised method in the delivery of the MWR message is personal selling. All food and hospitality personnel should be knowledgeable about what other activities have to offer. When a patron visits one activity, there should be information available that makes the patron aware of other activities. Many commands have the MWR Director or other staff member brief personnel at welcome aboard or training briefs. These are perfect opportunities to not only talk about what food and hospitality offers, but also to "sell" the entire program.

Personal selling leaves a lasting impression because of the person-to-person contact. The main implication of personal selling is that each employee must be activity and patron oriented, and must make every effort to provide the patron with efficient, friendly, courteous service. Skillful personal selling is not something that can be taught to an employee easily-it is an attitude. But it is something that can be influenced through training and good staff relations.

It is impossible to have good personal selling if the management and staff are not proud of their activity and its services. Management cannot expect the staff to be sales people unless they have a good reason to be proud of their work. It is a combination, therefore, of both the management and the staff that accounts for successful selling. Each must accept personal responsibility for promoting the club in the course of their daily job related activities.

Public Speaking

Public speaking offers another opportunity to sell your activity. Presentations to wives' clubs, incoming Marines, and at social functions can inform, influence, and stimulate interest in MWR activities. The use of slides, movies, and other visual cues can enhance the effectiveness of the presentation. The person speaking should be well prepared and keep the presentation well paced and interesting. Let all base activities and local organisations know you are available as a speaker.

Private and base organisations may welcome you as a speaker at their meetings, especially if you have an exhibit or demonstration to present. Outreach to the local community provides an excellent opportunity to get acquainted and become knowledgeable about local demographics. Briefings should be given periodically to all commands, staff personnel, appropriate clubs, and base organisations.

Promotional Media

Various forms of media can be used to promote and communicate your program or a promotion to potential patrons. Some of the most important are as follows:

— *Brochures:* Brochures can provide patrons information about food and hospitality activities, facilities, and services. A brochure may be current for a limited duration, such as one which promotes a specific promotion; or it may be timeless, such as one which indicates facility location, hours of operation, services offered, etc.

  There is a wide variety of creative ideas which can be used when developing brochures. Some helpful guidelines are:

  — Use two color paper for interest and black ink for impact.

  — Medium weight paper is more impressive than light weight.

  — Consider the different paper textures available, such as matte or glossy.

— Bi-fold and three-fold are the most common type of folds used.

— Photos create interest.

— Areas of white space encourage reading.

— Set off headlines by using larger type and/or different typefaces, such as bold and italics.

— Indent paragraphs.

— *Flyers:* Should be thought of as miniature posters that highlight important details of a program, service, or activity. Key elements to consider in developing an effective flyer are:

— Accuracy

— Quality

— Logo

— White space

— Who, What, Where, When, Why, and How

— Large letters for easy reading

— Rub-on letters instead of a felt pen

— Blowup of photo for background

— Silk screening

Remember to remove all brochures and posters when they become out-of-date.

— *Marquees:* Marquees, billboards, and signs are on duty 24 hours a day and are an excellent complement to existing advertising. One of the primary considerations in setting up a billboard or marquee is location. Criteria for determining placement:

— Length of unobstructed view. When does the sign become fully visible from a car?

— Type of traffic. Fast? Slow?

— Does the sign face oncoming or outgoing traffic?

— Immediate surroundings. Are there traffic lights, competing signs, buildings?

— Size and physical appeal of the sign.

— Patrons to be reached. Do you want to contact patrons going to or from work?

Marquees must be easy to read. Keep the message short-eight words or less and if possible include the MWR logo. Marquees are usually read as the patron is moving, so they must say only one thing and say it clearly. The clarity and aesthetics are also important in telling the patron what type of operation you have. A good looking sign connotes a quality operation. A key element relating to the patron's awareness is keeping the message on the marquee current. Messages should be changed every few days to keep the patron's interest. Old messages result in patrons losing interest and reduces the overall effectiveness of the marquee.

— *Posters:* Posters should be large, eye-catching, and easy to read and understand. Produce enough to distribute to all base activities, and if possible, post outside as well as inside. Place the posters in high-traffic areas, and if there are no bulletin boards available, use easels to display your message.

— *Activity Calendars:* Send calendars to target groups featuring activities they are most likely to participate in. This is an excellent means of providing patrons with a long-range schedule of upcoming events, programs, etc.

— *Audio Visuals:* Videotapes, slide shows, and other visual media can effectively present your message. These can be used for welcome aboard briefs, command cable television, base community meetings (such as wives' clubs), or as movie trailers at the base theater. Audio visuals should be made available to every pertinent activity, both on and off base.

— *Other Visuals:* Banners are excellent for advertising upcoming events. Hang them in high traffic areas such as main gates and use large letters on both sides and consider silk-screening, hand lettering, and Velcro letters. Bus Cards used inside base buses, similar to those seen in subways and on commercial buses, are effective because they have a captive audience. Signs on the back and sides of MWR vehicles will attract attention. Exhibits presenting a specific activity are an excellent way to elicit interest and attract new patrons. For example, an appealing, eye-catching exhibit about your activity and located in the exchange area, can encourage people to visit your activity. Buttons, T-shirt messages, table tents, menu clip-ons, and messages on place mats, napkins, and coasters will call attention to your activity message. Work with other base facilities to get your message to their patrons and participants.

— *Telephone Hot Lines:* You can designate a special number to call for information about MWR activities. All announcements on the pre-recorded telephone message should include upcoming events, discount information, MWR news, local entertainment, schedules, etc. If you use a recorded message, make sure the information is current. Make sure there is someone available to answer calls and the line is relatively free from other types of incoming calls. Publicise the number as much as possible.

— *Direct Mailings:* The greatest advantage of direct mail advertising is that it will reach the intended market. For direct mail advertising purposes, you can strive to reach your basic markets. Your basic markets are: active duty Marines and their families, retired military, reservists in your area, and other eligible MWR patrons, such as civilians who work on base. From a direct mail standpoint the markets do not need to be further segmented. The effectiveness of direct mail advertising depends on current lists and addresses of potential and current patrons. This includes timely information for all Recent arrivals. As an example you may want to send a personalised welcome aboard letter. The letter should be sent to newly arrived Marines and their families, inviting them to visit food and hospitality activities. It could serve as the only nice individualised touch that the newcomer receives.

Many other types of information can be communicated through direct mail; such as special promotions, menus, parties, and entertainment. It is important that direct mail advertisements be kept separate from the monthly newsletter since the advertisement loses its effectiveness when it accompanies regularly delivered material.

Direct mail advertisements should be creative, professionally presented, and informative. The date, time, location, price, and other necessary information describing the special promotions should always be included. It is also a good idea to have the promoter (manager, chef, assistant) personally sign the direct mail advertisement before mailing. This adds a special extra touch. It becomes a personal invitation rather than a general invitation.

There are three major concerns associated with direct mail advertising. First, care should be taken not to overstuff direct mail advertisements with more than one or two promotions. The more stuffing, the less likelihood of its being read. Second, care must be taken to personalise the mail as much as possible (i.e., ink signed letter versus stamped); and third, the material should be professional in appearance. The cost of direct mail advertising may be one of the most effective advertising expenditures that an activity can make. It is sent specifically to the primary patron and is utilised only when something special is being promoted. Each food and hospitality manager should incorporate direct mail advertising into the marketing budget.

— *Newspapers:* The base paper is perhaps the most effective method of communication used by MWR activities. At many installations, MWR writes their own news releases and provides the information to Public Affairs. Well written newspaper articles usually describe what the activity is, where it will be held, when it will take place, what the cost will be, and to whom the services are directed. The first paragraph of the news release should include information such as who, what, why, when, and where. Use "how" in the second paragraph if it will not fit easily into the first. News releases are cut away from the bottom up by editors, so make the first paragraph the most substantive and the last paragraph the least important, with the others providing information and data to support the lead paragraph. Use only as much material as will fit on one sheet of paper, double space, with one inch wide margins. Use clear, concise language and get to the point. If possible, use a quote from a dignitary, an official or a base officer to lend creditability and another angle to stories. The newspaper can expand the story by calling the appropriate contact person for more information.

— *MWR Supplements:* Supplements are an excellent means of providing informative articles and ads to a widespread audience. This publication is produced periodically and provides readers with an in-depth look at a particular program, special event, discount attraction, etc.

Customer Service Policies

An important element of promotion that cannot be overlooked is customer service. Food and hospitality can advertise and promote its services extensively, but if there is no customer service program then promotional efforts will be in vain. Vital to the success of any MWR activity is the customer oriented attitude of employees. Customer service policies must start with the activity manager. Policies should be communicated to employees and supported by them. These policies and practices must become an integral part of the food and hospitality operation.

A key management philosophy which should be practiced in every food and hospitality program is the assumption that the customer is right unless a complaint is proven unjustified. Patrons who take the time to lodge complaints believe they have legitimate problems. Ignoring or responding negatively to complaints will result in nothing but ill will. These customers deserve prompt attention, ideally, inquiries should be responded to on the same day they are received.

Giving your customers what they want and need to make them happy pays great dividends. Happy customers tell their friends-approximately 72 percent of first-time customers come because of recommendations. Conversely, unhappy customers tell at least 10 other people.

Quick resolution of patron complaints lets patrons know they are important and also lessens the possibility of the complaint being aired to others. By being open to customer criticism, we develop an effective means to measure how we are serving our patrons. It is essential that food and hospitality build an effective customer service program. This starts with training employees on proper ways to respond to customer complaints. The wrong response to a customer's problem can create a negative effect which ripples when dissatisfied patrons spread their complaints.

Employees should be personable, have a neat appearance, a good telephone voice, patience, and a knowledge of the food and hospitality program. Above all, they must have a genuine interest in people. A dedicated, responsive, customer-oriented organisation is one of the best contributions that can be made in this climate of heightened customer awareness.

Visual Merchandising

Visual merchandising helps distinguish food and hospitality activities from other activities on or off base. When well planned, visual merchandising can help boost sales. It encompasses all aspects of activity services, including areas not typically considered income producers or sales related.

Merchandising helps make each patron's visit to the activity a memorable one, provides a unique atmosphere, and makes the entire facility more attractive, pleasant, and comfortable. Any area within the activity which can achieve these goals must be considered a potential merchandising area.

The following deserve particular attention with respect to merchandising efforts:

— Menus and Food

— Services

— Facilities

— Pricing of Services

— Uniforms

— Entertainment

Within each of these areas there are particular focuses of attention. Combined, the overall goal is the activity image, which is the way patrons perceive the activity and its services. Although the definition implies that image is an individual opinion, there are several ways the activity manager can present the club so that its image is consistent for all patrons.

Merchandising can influence the patron's perception of the activity (i.e., how it looks, its comforts, its friendliness). In fact, merchandising may be the single most important factor in affecting the patron's perception. The awareness of image-related areas deserves constant managerial attention.

Menus and Food

If the activity's primary purpose is to provide food and beverage, the menu and food are the most important areas where an image can be created. The entire activity perception can be affected by a poor or unimaginative menu. The areas within the menu that deserve merchandising attention are the use of colors, graphics, printing styles, cover design, menu item descriptive wording, size and shape of menu, and the actual choice of menu items.

Again, merchandising means providing distinctive qualities and special touches. The menu should be designed creatively and printed by a professional printer. The use of seasonal menus allows for merchandising through graphics and/or color schemes which depict seasonal activities. Menus also allow the activity manager to develop specialty dishes and merchandise them as such on the menu. Certain menu items can be emphasised and merchandised through descriptive wording. There are no limits to the usefulness of the menu in helping provide a distinctive and memorable food and beverage operation.

Food quality must reach the level of expectation created by the menu. The actual taste of the food will linger on longer, and have a much more lasting effect on the patrons' perception of the food service, than the menu. The two, the menu and the food, must be thought of as a team, with food quality being the more important consideration.

Although good food quality will compensate for a poor menu, a good menu will not compensate for poor food quality. The ultimate goal is a menu that complements food quality and vice versa. The importance of food quality as a merchandising tool is exemplified by the fact that word-of-mouth advertising is critical to the success of an activity's food operation. Merchandising the food operations through good quality food turns the patron who has had an enjoyable dining experience into an advertising medium.

Services: Services can be defined as any service offered to the patron, whether it be for profit or not. Services include food and beverages, party facilities, meeting rooms, recreational areas and/or equipment, entertainment, and other services such as telephones in Temporary Lodging Facility rooms, newspapers, and vending machines. As can be seen, there are countless areas within services where merchandising can be a factor. Merchandising services means emphasising any special services, facilities and/or capabilities. A pool room, for instance, represents a multitude of possibilities for merchandising. Special "sharp shooter" nights, tournaments, trick shooter exhibitions and partner tournaments are only a few possibilities that turn an ordinary pool room into a potential profit producer.

Managers should evaluate their facilities in respect to potential services merchandising. Other areas which deserve consideration are recreational activities (pinball, ping pong, tennis, golf), food and beverage service (specialty ethnic nights, family nights, "all you can eat" nights), and entertainment (concerts, talent shows, dancing exhibitions, dinner shows). The key point is that there are endless ways in which activity services can be merchandised. The following steps are important in merchandising services.

— Determine exactly what services are available.

— Determine what types of services can be made available with or without capital expenditures.

— Establish a priority list of services which should be merchandised based upon market questionnaires, intuition, and informal patron surveys.

— Develop a list for each service or promotions and events which can be implemented and specially merchandised. Be sure to make them realistic and affordable.

— Establish a rough plan as to when these types of services can be offered.

Facilities

The actual condition of the activity facility is one area that is not an income producer but is, nonetheless, an area that deserves merchandising attention. A very clean, well-organised, and appealing facility will most definitely affect the patron's perception of the activity as a whole. Therefore, as previously emphasised, facilities are included in areas affecting image and should be treated as areas requiring merchandising efforts.

Some of the areas that require attention are the exterior grounds, landscape, entrance ways, hallways, carpeting, furniture, decorations, and meeting rooms. In addition, food and beverage facilities (dining rooms, bars), recreational areas, and entertainment facilities all require the same focus.

Examples of the type of merchandising that helps promote services are well-landscaped and well-maintained lawns, gardens, shrubbery, and sidewalk areas; clean and well-painted entrance ways, awnings and doors; and well-maintained carpets, woodwork, lighting fixtures, and hallway furniture. The patron who arrives at the facility and notices a well-kept and well-structured garden is seeing a merchandising effort aimed at providing appealing and attractive facilities. Conversely, an improperly maintained garden or entrance way does not help to create a favorable image.

Another example of the facility's role in merchandising is the maintenance of meeting and special function rooms. These rooms should be attractive, well-decorated and clean. The patrons using the rooms will feel more comfortable in a well-maintained meeting room and will notice the efforts to personalise the room for their functions, such as providing special decorations for weddings and parties. Again, this all helps create an overall favorable image for the activity.

Pricing of Services

Pricing is not considered a typical merchandising tool. Its primary objective is to provide income. It must be assumed, however, that the patron views pricing as a very important aspect of services. Value is the key. Providing value becomes a marketing/merchandising effort. Throughout the private sector, value is a very strongly emphasised quality in advertising and merchandising programs.

Fixed prices, (room rates, menu prices, drink prices) are not as amenable to merchandising considerations as are special events and promotions. Special entertainment such as concerts and various types of exhibitions, special dinner nights, and holiday parties present opportunities for price merchandising.

Uniforms

It is necessary to mention uniforms as a merchandising tool because they are considered a basic part of an activity's "ambiance." A well-dressed employee is one of the best merchandising tools we have. An entire staff of well-dressed employees is the ultimate goal. Uniforms, like landscaping, provide an immediate visual experience to the patron. Poorly organised and unkempt uniforms create an unfavorable image of the activity as a whole, even though they are not considered income producers or services. Uniforms should be provided to all employees, or a standard uniform should be established so that all employees may purchase similar attire. Whenever possible, uniforms should reflect the central theme of the facility. This is another way by which distinctiveness and image are created.

Entertainment

Entertainment is the one which continually utilises merchandising as a primary sales tool. Merchandising efforts should concentrate on personal selling, advertising, and the actual choice of entertainment. Obviously, the more familiar or more popular the entertainment, the more distinctive the activity becomes. Entertainment should always be viewed as a special activity deserving special promotional considerations.

Entertainment needs merchandising efforts to stimulate interest. It is self-defeating to offer the same kind of entertainment over and over again-its special qualities become lost. This may not be the case for very popular entertainment such as a special band that always draws big crowds, but generally, too much repetition of one form of entertainment nullifies the merchandising aspects of the event.

Some merchandising-type tools which are used for promoting entertainment are phrases such as "appearing for the first time ever," "back by popular demand," "all the way from (name of place)," and "command performance." Each of these phrases, and similar phrases, are attempts to emphasise uniqueness and distinctiveness. There can be no substitute for merchandising; it offers an opportunity for the activity to impress patrons with its attention to details. Perhaps the most important outgrowth of good merchandising, however, is that not only do patrons benefit from management's commitment to provide special touches, but the activity also benefits from increased patron participation.

Effective Marketing Planning Process

Planning is essential to the success of any business. The marketing planning process attempts to organise thinking about the future, what must be accomplished, and when it must be done. Since most management problems happen on a day-to-day basis, most managers focus only on the present. Long-range planning to these managers is next week.

An effective planning process is to your best advantage. A marketing plan will provide you with a blueprint for making important business decisions. The process requires a thorough evaluation of your activity, and upon completion you will have outlined your business's specific goals, strategies, programs, and budget. This will provide a rational, logical sense of direction for your activity and detail your strategy for success. Among the benefits to be realised are: A sense of direction that is rational and logical.

— Coordinated effort and maximised use of resources.

— Indexes to measure and evaluate how the organisation is doing.

— Improved public relations allowing better interpretation of the organisation's goals and achievements.
— Increased employee involvement.
— Improved staff capabilities to manage and assess overall program operations.
— Increased foresight in terms of meeting future community needs and operation requirements, thereby reducing crisis management.

Although the Food and Hospitality Director and the activity level manager can tell you what they would like to do, often nothing is written-no objectives, no tasking, no milestone dates. As a result, many activities are at a level of stagnation, with no visible improvements patrons can relate to, no lessons learned for improvement, and in some instances, no new equipment for improving the activities.

Some of the most common statements from managers who do not prepare written plans are:

— Business techniques cannot be used in nonprofit organisations.
— Day-to-day crises need attention, leaving little time for planning.
— Efforts that require thinking about the future are difficult and uncertain.
— Managers have never been trained in the planning process.

Planning is both strategic and operational. This section focuses on strategic planning which is primarily concerned with long-range issues, such as the mix of products within a product portfolio. A mix of products in different stages of the life cycle is also an aspect of strategic planning. Diversifying a menu would be an example of this. "Fad" items will generate substantial profits, but have a limited life cycle compared to more stable items. An example would be a popular appetiser item as compared to the ever-popular cheeseburger. The marketing planning process requires you to consider the wants and needs of your customers, or that the process be market driven. In researching and developing your plan, your experience and customers will be invaluable resources. Other suggested personnel to consult include your:

— MWR Marketing Personnel

— Installation Commander

— Installation Sergeant Major

— Base Master Planner

— Other Food and Hospitality Activity Managers

The following are important principles to consider when developing a marketing plan.

— The process of planning should be done by outlining your steps before beginning the process.

— Relevant planning involves fact finding and analysis.

— Planning is a continuous process and the primary responsibility of management.

— Planning is more than a staff process and requires obtaining input from your customers and other food and hospitality managers, and taking into account your competition and experience.

— Groups and/or individuals who are directly affected by planning decisions should have the opportunity to influence these decisions at appropriate points during the planning process.

— Persons accountable for implementing plans should be involved in the planning.

— Related tasks should be grouped to determine if they will support a common objective.

— Tasks should be clear and accurate.

To develop a marketing plan, you must:

1. Examine your current marketing situation.
   a. Identify trends and examine your local environment.
   b. Examine potential opportunities and threats to your program.
   c. Determine the strengths and weaknesses of your program.
   d. Ask yourself: "What business am I in?"
   e. Identify who your patrons are and what they need.
2. Set objectives and goals for your marketing plan.
3. Determine the best marketing strategy.
   a. Determine target markets.
   b. Develop the best marketing mix.
   c. Complete a competitive analysis.
4. Develop a plan of action.
5. Determine a budget and set controls.
6. Develop an Executive Summary.

Service Quality Management

Service encounters are the building blocks of quality hospitality service. How can hospitality businesses manage them more effectively? Here we suggest a two step process in the evaluation of a service chain.

First, hospitality managers should identify each encounter in the chain that they wish to take apart, and then single out those that are of operational or strategic significance – in effect, focusing in on the few encounters that really make a difference to guest experience and thus to the bottom line.

Second, apply what we have called the 6 S's to improving these critical encounters through effective redesign.

Hospitality service encounters run the gamut from those that are very trivial to those that are highly critical. They vary greatly in their nature and may be simple or complex, standard or custom, low tech or high tech, remote or friendly, low or high skill, frequent or occasional, and so on. They can be instrumental dealing with the performance of necessary utilitarian activities or can involve emotion-laden hospitality events.

An initial management task is to understand a service encounter by discerning and dealing with those attributes that are most important to guests. In doing so, pertinent questions must be raised about the specific service encounter(s) under consideration. With respect to a particular service encounter, hospitality managers might raise many questions like the following:

— Exactly what happened?

— What were the guest reactions?

— Should it be done differently?

— What resources would assure optimal performance?

— What changes should be made?

— How can such changes best be put into effect?

The specific encounter(s) under consideration will, of course, indicate the kinds of questions that should be pursued. It is important to obtain adequate information to understand the situation thoroughly. Determining the context of a situation relating to a hospitality encounter that has gone wrong establishes parameters for improvement.

All this is part of the second step. With the information at hand hospitality managers can organise, and analyse the data and it is here that the 6S approach can help. These are:

— Specification
— Staff
— Space
— System
— Support
— Style

Specification means clearly detailing information about the what, when, where, and how, of service encounters. It requires giving careful thought to the linkages between particular service encounters and others in the service chain.

The starting point for hospitality service encounter analysis is specifying clearly the overall service strategy and what it is designed to achieve. Is the purpose cost or service quality leadership? Is it to provide unique service values, customised or standardised, complex or simple, frequent or occasional? Is it to provide service at any reasonable cost? Is service limited to a luxury package, or does it include budget travellers?

Which staff members are involved in providing the service? What skills do they need? What training has been provided? How committed are they to service goals? Is team cooperation or individual empowerment required? What attitudes are appropriate— friendly, open, helpful, warm service, or efficient, unobtrusive, uninvolving, unthreatening service? What staff members deal with guests? How close are the 'backroom' staff to guests? Are staff presentations and appearances appropriate?

To what extent are guests involved in the provision of service? What skill, knowledge, information, or experience do guests need to fulfill their roles? What are likely guest expectations? What communication occurred between guest and service provider? Did the dynamics of the exchange proceed smoothly? Do any language and cultural barriers exist?

Where will the service encounter occur? Is the space appropriately designed to facilitate the service encounter? Is there adequate space to handle each of the activities such as waiting, completing forms, storing or handling luggage, assembling tours? Is signage appropriate? Is the decor attractive to guests and supportive of activities that have to be carried out?

Are the necessary systems to support the encounter in place? Is the information necessary to respond effectively to guests' needs readily available? Is the appropriate technology being fully used? Are the interfaces between different functions such as housekeeping and front office, sales and front office, fully operational? What measurements of quality, or performance, are in use? Are they the most helpful for both service providers and managers? Are the criteria for success clearly defined? Is everyone involved aware of guest needs and concerns?

Are the service providers given the facilities and financial and human support needed to do the job? Is the technology appropriate? Have employees been given the training needed? Are incentive and reward systems geared to the tasks to be performed? Is supervision supportive? Does organisation structure help or hinder performance?Are the suggested procedures appropriate?

How should the service encounter be conducted, given the enterprise culture? Is the management style, and marketing orientation, appropriate for the tasks? Do service providers have the appropriate attitudes? Is the right emphasis being placed on service quality?

When hospitality managers have carried out this two step process they will be in an excellent position to make decisions that will both improve the quality of hospitality services provided and guest perceptions of them. Zeroing in on hospitality service quality in this manner will help hospitality businesses meet the service challenges of the millennium, enhance their market positions, and reap the associated profit rewards.

Service Quality and Competitiveness

A review of the theoretical models of business competitiveness reveals the significance of two kinds of factors in regard to this area - internal factors pertaining to the actual firm, and external factors related to the structure of the industry in which the firm operates as well as the economy of the country as a whole. Empirical evidence should corroborate these models by providing sufficient data to identify the relative significance of each individual factor regarding the global improvement of business competitiveness. However, most available studies are partial since they focus on quantifying the effects of macroeconomic variables, the effects of sector variables, or the effects of strictly business-oriented variables.

Quality of service has been one the most widely investigated factors among those strictly related to business. In this context, business competitiveness is positively related to matching the characteristics of the service to the ideal preferences of clients, i.e., their level of satisfaction. This fact reveals the key role of service quality on the improvement of business competitiveness, and how this has an effect not only outside the actual firm, but also on the variables within it. However, most relevant research on this issue deals with the theoretical study of the relationships that exist between quality and business competitiveness or with partial empirical relationships between variables. The aim of this matter is to analyse - from a global perspective - the main relationships existing between service quality and businesses competitiveness.

The data used to empirically verify this model were gathered from hotels owned by a national hotel company in Andalusia. The client survey carried out by the hotel - in the form of questionnaires - was the basis for creating the service quality indicators and establishing their most relevant dimensions. On the other hand, the economic and financial data pertaining to the hotels served to create competitiveness indicators for each of them. The results obtained were used to empirically verify a set of key hypotheses regarding the competitiveness of these hotels and to propose measures designed to improve this.

Cultural Dimensions of Hospitality Service

In the provision of hospitality service for international tourists, there are several kinds of culture at work. The first of these is the culture of service, that is, the values and meanings which give to service its essential quality. In a service encounter a tourist and a waiter (for example) engage in the culture of service and the waiter performs emotional labour in addition to performing technical skills. The actors in the service encounter bring to the interaction their own ethnic identities and engage in cross - cultural communication. To ensure the provision of appropriate hospitality service human resource development must take account of the cultural dimensions of hospitality.

For several years now the founding states of the Association of Southeast Asian nations (ASEAN) have made inbound international tourism an important economic activity. With their abundance of cultural and natural attractions they have lured tourists from a variety of culturally diverse generating regions. Great progress has been made since 1958 when Checci and Company, in association with the United States Depart of Commerce and pacific Area Travel Association, began an investigation of the potential for tourism in the Asia - pacific region.

At that time tourism in Indonesia was virtually non - existent. At the same time the Government of Singapore had eliminated its tourism program on the grounds that tourism was "frivolous" and "too vague" to be of use to the economy. According to the Checci Report, in 1959 the Thai government had only recently begun to see tourism as an important source of jobs, foreign exchange and income and had accordingly taken action by forming the Tourist Organisation of Thailand.

The pursuit of inbound tourism as a prominent component of national economic life has, in recent years, not been confined to the foundation members of ASEAN. While those states have continued to expand their frontiers of tourism to provide new attractions for tourists, other Southeast Asian states have begun to pursue economic diversification through international tourism.

For various reasons these states, until recently, had not been prime destinations for travellers. For more than two decades Myanmar's pursuit of the isolationist Burmese Way to Socialism deprived international tourists of the chance of extended stay during which to experience the country's cultural and natural attractions. Now Myanmar seeks tourists to enhance its economic positions ant its international reputation.

Another perhaps surprising newcomer to the business of attracting tourists is the conservative oil-rich Islamic state of Brunei which according to Roger Mitton, is in the process of becoming a 'hip tourist destination' in order to diversify its economy. Mitton reports that the sultanate is 'loosening up' in order to become 'a fun place to visit.'

Vietnam and Laos are also now open for tourist business after years of Cold War conflict and economic rigidity. Their Indochinese neighbour, Cambodia, was identified by the Checchi Report as the single greatest potential tourist attraction in Southeast Asia because of the remains of the Khmer civilisation at Angkor. Unfortunately, however, continued political instability, by creating a perception of danger, so far prevents it from realising its full potential as a tourist destination. According to Kim, international tourism growth in the Asia - Pacific region is anticipated to rise to approximately 200 million visitor arrivals by the year 2000. It should come as no surprise, therefore, that the tourism and hospitality industry will be a major employer of labour.

Need for Quality Service

According to the World Travel and Tourism Council (WTTC) the Asia Pacific region's tourism industry is still in its infancy and therefore the full impact of tourism is yet to be realised. Whilst tourism growth in the region provides cause for optimism, it has already created labour supply problems for employers. By 2004, Metzger estimates that 122 million jobs will be created in Asia alone and if a consistently high level of service is to be maintained across all sectors of the industry, some 122 million skilled workers will have to be found to deliver tourism service.

Economically, much is at stake in the region if its service providers fail to meet the demands of its tourists. For example, the gross output in Thailand for 1996 from tourism was estimated to be 8.5 billion United States dollars. Due to continuing economic uncertainties in Thailand, tourism authorities are likely to seek an increase in this figure due to the need for additional foreign exchange.

Although current economic conditions in Japan are affecting outbound tourism in that country resulting in more Japanese taking their holiday at home, nevertheless Ilakim believes that, so far as outbound Japanese tourism is concerned, the majority of the jobs catering for their needs will be in the customer contact area. It is here that there will be a need for host countries in the Asia-Pacific region to have customer contact people who can communicate effectively and sensitively with the Japanese.

According to Yee the competitive edge of an economy is not found in its commodities or low wage labour, but in the contribution of a rising quality labour which can provide high levels of service. Thus the notion of quality service will play a crucial role in the economic contribution of tourism and hospitality to the region. As quality service is possibly the foremost determinant of success in the tourism and hospitality business it is important that the focus be placed on improving service. If more tourists are to be attracted to the region, it is imperative that the strategy is not put in jeopardy by the lack of quality service. It is, however, one thing to identify the need for quality service, but it is entirely another matter as to how such a service might be supplied.

The tourism and hospitality industry in the Asia Pacific region has an image problem which results in government, employers and prospective employees all sharing reservations about the nature of the industry itself. For example, the industry is perceived by potential employees as being dominated by expatriate staff in its key managerial and professional positions thereby offering limited career opportunities to the domestic work force. It is also perceived as offering low status employment for young adults or marginally skilled workers, a situation which may well lead governments to conclude that it is a minor player in the economic life of a countr. Its poor image as an employer is reinforced when students undertake work experience during their industry placements.

Certain lessons might be drawn for the region from the Hong Kong experience. Yee reports that in Hong Kong some students in tourism and hospitality are so negatively affected by their hotel placement that they choose not to enter the industry because they feel they are being used as cheap labour or as fodder for the operational needs of the hotel.

Cultural differences are demonstrated in a variety of ways. In some societies, for example, great respect is accorded to age to a degree not evident in other societies. Ideas about personal space vary from culture to culture. In some cultures, making eye contact during verbal communication is unacceptable; in other cultures eye contact is important as a sign of openness. These various examples of cultural difference are generalisations. Besides belonging to cultural groups people are also unique personalities. Uniqueness does not, however, diminish the importance of culture. According to Singer 'uniqueness does know bounds'; these bounds are set by the cultural groups with which individuals identify.

While language differences are likely to be the most obvious component of cross- cultural service encounters, there are other aspects of Hofstede's 'software of the mind' that need to be taken into account. For example, what 'collective programming of the mind' has taken place to influence the attitude of a young man or woman towards the desirability of being a waiter in a restaurant?

Anecdotal evidence from Southeast Asian tourism and hospitality students in Australia suggests that such a job is not considered desirable for its own sake. Instead it is seen as a way to make money for immediate living expenses and, in the long term, as a springboard for a managerial position. In some cases there is reluctance to learn what are considered to be the more menial hospitality skills. If the job is not highly regarded within the cultural group, how will this affect the waiter's enthusiasm for and performance in the job? There is also the likelihood that the 'collective programming of the mind' has included animosity between cultural groups.

Will this animosity affect the service encounters between members of those groups?

Yuan highlights the major issues associated with the cultural dimensions of service. The service received in a host country is often judged by the tourist's own cultural standards. For example, the Asia Pacific region is host to approximately 10 million Japanese tourists each year. According to Jang there is a great chance that visitors to the region will find customer contact people either unaware of or unable to respond to their clients' needs.

Tourists in foreign lands are likely to be in search of cultural knowledge and experience. Whilst this knowledge and experience is formally provided by tour operators and guides they employ, informally hospitality service providers such as waiters and receptionists may, through conversations with guests, serve as another source of cultural knowledge.

Anecdotal evidence from tourists who have visited Bali, for example, indicates service encounters in restaurants during which young Balinese waiters, anxious to practise their English, engage with guests in the exchange of knowledge about their respective cultures. In some cases friendships are formed, correspondence is exchanged and contacts are renewed on repeat visits to Bali.

In the anthropological literature, the waiter performing this role is described as a culture broker. According to social anthropologist, Naomi Brown, 'culture brokers are found in all cross-cultural situations ... amongst taxi drivers, tourist guides, tourist police, security guards, hotel workers and market vendors. They act as mediators between tourists and the resident population'. In this capacity they play an important part in enhancing the tourists' experience of a destination.

HRD and Hospitality Service Provision

Human Resource Development has improved performance as its ultimate goal in order to enhance the competitiveness and efficiency of an organisation. The term HRD is made up of three core components:

— training to improve the performance of employees in their current job,

— education to develop the whole person for future roles and responsibilities which as yet remain unknown, and

— development which prepares people for their responsibilities in the short to medium term of their career.

As tourism and hospitality is one of the largest and fastest growing industries in the world, it has, in the view of the WTTC, a need to address increased and improved tourism education in the region. This step is necessary in order to accommodate and adapt to ever increasing pressure on tourism and hospitality resources in the region. According to Yee HRD is one of the most widely used terms in Asia-Pacific gatherings because it is seen as central to the competitive edge of the economy of a nation.

The key HRD stakeholders in any country are its HRD providers, supporters and users in terms of government, employers, and educational institutions. Tourists also are indirectly stakeholders in that they receive the benefit or otherwise of the outcomes and effectiveness of HRD initiatives. Governments will not become involved in HRD initiatives unless they believe tourism can make a positive contribution to their economy. As tourism employs 1 in 9 of the work force of the world, and it is predicted by 2005 to contribute some 2.0 trillion dollars from travel and gross output in the Asia Pacific region. it would seem good economic sense for government to support well constructed arguments for quality improvements in the industry.

Ideally the development of a program for skills development should be a joint project for industry and vocational education which together bring to the task an understanding of the requirements of industry and an appreciation of the pedagogical factors involved in providing training for skills development. The refinement of competency- based modules and train the trainer programs in recent years means that standardised training can take place in vocational education institutions and in the workplace through on - the -job training.

Within the domain of skills development, there i5 the opportunity to empower employees by engaging them in a process of commitment to quality service When skills are applied within a Quality framework, these can be used to achieve satisfying service outcomes. If employees are engaged actively in continually improving their service processes to meet the needs of their customers, hospitality service provision will be the beneficiary.

For example, through their direct contact with customers in a bar, hospitality staff may become aware that long queues form no matter how expertly they perform their skills. Because of their first-hand knowledge of the situation, bar staff, if consulted, may recommend a change to the work process such as a series of minibars within the establishment to reduce time pressures on staff and satisfy their customers. In this instance both the customer and staff experience satisfying outcomes.

Developing a Culture of Service

Competency-based modules for skills development cannot guarantee the inculcation of the values which underpin the culture of service. Customer relations modules, through role play methodology, may attempt to develop behaviours which are supposed to indicate a commitment to the emotional content of service but such behaviours are mere surface acting and may lack the ring of sincerity.

While there are good reasons for the 'stereotyped forms of address' and the programmed presentation of service in fast food restaurants, it is unlikely that many customers take the performance seriously. Crang likens the performance of emotional labour to a theatrical event directed by management. While surface acting training is one means of preparing people for their roles as service-givers, Crang also draws attention to staff training 'in a deeper Stanislavskian level of performance', that is, deep acting which, if Hochschild's view is accepted, can have a psychologically damaging effect upon the performers because they lose touch with their true feelings. If acting, either surface or deep, is inappropriate, how then can a truly genuine culture of service be developed?

At the level of management in a hospitality enterprise there must be a genuine appreciation of the values underlying the culture of service and an understanding of what constitutes a positive total experience for guests.

This genuine appreciation is reflected in the manner in which staff are recruited with attention being given to the recruitment of people with personality characteristics suitable for empathetic service provision. It is also reflected in the culture of the organisation which creates 'a sense of enrichment in the job'. These criteria for appropriate management have implications for the education of managers who, besides needing studies in business and management, would have a greater understanding of the importance of the psychosocial dimensions of hospitality provision through in-depth study of relevant social sciences such as sociology and psychology. This understanding would encompass both the psychosocial dimensions of the tourist experience as well as the need for protection of the psychological well-being of the service workers from the deleterious effects of emotional labour.

Appreciation of Cultural Diversity

The hospitality worker is likely to work in a multicultural environment. Besides the cross-cultural encounters front of house, there are also back of house encounters which have their own cultural dimension. While globalisation may result in superficial cultural homogenisation, the strength of traditional values and attitudes developed over many centuries should not be underestimated. The Chinese chef, for example, is the end result of a long established Confucian tradition which is not shared by the Irish waiter. Each is the product of a particular cultural programming.

How should hospitality workers be prepared for interactions with a multicultural clientele and a multicultural workforce? Within current hospitality education and training programs one may find components relating to cross-cultural communication. The danger with short courses such as these is that they will highlight the apparently exotic aspects of a culture and thus encourage stereotyping and ridicule.

Cross-cultural understanding may be best achieved by a long-term systematic development of cultural knowledge beginning in elementary school. Such an education should highlight humanity's shared experiences as well as cultural diversity and should span all the years of one's education.

Hospitality as an Occupation

Generally service work in hospitality has low status as an occupation. At the same time the customer contact aspect of hospitality, it has been argued, plays an important role in the total tourist experience. It therefore seems imperative to take steps to raise the status of the occupation.

One way in which an attempt can be made to achieve this goal is through educational provision for careers in hospitality. While considerable attention has been given to management training, more attention needs to be given to the integration of operational training into educational programs at degree level. There are, no doubt, several ways in which this can be achieved. For example, a degree may be constructed by building a one or two-year program at university on to a two-year program at vocational college. Alternatively, a three or four-year degree program may be taken concurrently with a hospitality program at a vocational college. The latter approach has the advantage of introducing students to the culture of academic reflection from the beginning of tertiary study.

In university circles it is likely that combining vocational and academic study within a degree program will meet with some disapproval. The old status division between working with the hands and working with the mind has not disappeared. The combination of the two strands within a degree program, however, has many advantages. It supports an integrated career path for hospitality workers thus helping to overcome the perception that hospitality work is a dead-end job. It enables students who, through a relatively poor academic performance at school, did not gain entrance to university to prove their capabilities at vocational college and then to have a second chance at a university education. Lifelong learning cannot be constrained by artificial structures in education. In the vocational college component of the degree, assuming that hospitality practitioners are employed as teachers, it puts students in touch with the 'real world' of hospitality.

Self Service in Hospitality

This section makes the case for widespread deployment of self-service technologies and processes in the hospitality industry. Spurred by the success of airline check-in kiosks and seeking additional ways to cut costs and increase guest satisfaction, hoteliers will drive these solutions into properties aggressively.

Let's examine the potential impact of self service on the hospitality industry. First, an effective solution could yield significant savings through reduced front desk staffing levels. While the savings potential is greatest for large full-service or convention hotels, limited service could benefit as well, depending on the degree to which operators are willing to make the channel the primary mode of checking in. It is constructive here to note that although the airlines were at first reluctant, they have since achieved considerable savings.

Second, and perhaps more important, these solutions could increase guest satisfaction, especially for those who are inclined to self-empowerment. While the convenience of self service—eliminating or reducing lines at check-in and check-out, especially during peak periods—will appeal to many, the real power lies in what these solutions do for employees. No longer tethered to the front desk staring at a computer screen, front-line service staff can refocus on value-added guest interactions. In addition, engineered correctly, the technology can more consistently recognise guests and offer them personalised service commensurate with their value to the hotel. Automated concierge applications will allow guests to find the information they seek easily and quickly. We anticipate that this feature will have wide-scale applicability in limited-service hotels.

Third, hotels can expect revenue uplift beyond that offered by the increased wallet share of repeat guests. The opportunity exists to consistently up-sell room categories based on yield parameters. Many airlines offer first class upgrades (typically $50 for short/medium-haul domestic trips) at check-in based on availability and have seen incremental revenue. Additionally, kiosks are also an excellent channel to make dynamic one-to-one marketing offers, such as spa, restaurant and local attraction tie-ins.

Training and development

As hospitality organisations plan for the training and development of their employees in the future, they will evidently need to work more on their planning process - the current view is fairly negative. While just over two-thirds of respondents agreed that their training plan was 'effective', only 18 percent could "strongly agree" with such a statement. And one-third of respondents either took no position or viewed their plan as ineffective responses which suggest plenty of room for improvement.

As to training methods - "on the job" appears to be the dominant theme, although this approach should diminish somewhat in the future. Three out of four report using mentoring and coaching today with plans to increase this in the future. Just over 70 percent report formal classroom training, and two-thirds report video-based methods with plans to significantly increase this latter form in the future. Thankfully, there is also clear evidence of a significant increase in investment in training in the future - 89 percent of our respondents report plans to increase their training budgets, with well over one -quarter of these reporting that such increases will be significant.

The direction of such expanded investments in training, however, remains of concern. Just over three quarters of our respondents report the development and use of their own training programs, suggesting that our industry probably wastes a great amount of effort in duplication. By contrast, only 18 percent report the use of "pre - packaged" industry wide training programs. We conclude here that the industry's leadership and its educators should devote more attention to this area in the future - providing more in the way of generic training solutions with industry-wide application.

Hospitality organisations also use a variety of methods to identify workplace issues and for the most part intend to significantly increase their use in the future. Employee surveys, currently used by 70 percent of respondents, are planned for an increase in the future (by 79 percent). And while 68 percent of respondents acknowledge the use of suggestion boxes - the "employee" equivalent of the guest comment card - use of these passive instruments is expected to decline in the future.

Improving Performance

As human capital becomes more expensive to recruit, train and develop, increasing attention is being devoted to those factors that affect productivity. Empowerment, education, training, recognition programs and technology will all play different roles in this area in the future. The area with greatest prospective impact on productivity appears not surprisingly, to be training (cited by 94 percent). Three out of four respondents held that empowerment, education, career advancement, incentive and recognition programs would also have strong impacts on productivity in the future. Somewhat less impactful (although still indicated by a relatively high 70 percent of respondents), was the role of technology.

Following the identification of those factors that will contribute to productivity improvement in the future, we were interested in determining how productivity had changed, if at all, over the last three years. The results were surprising. No fewer than 22 percent of our respondents reported a decline in productivity. The Americas were the big standout with 29 percent of respondents reporting reduced productivity, while 14 percent and 13 percent respectively of respondents from EMEIA and Asia / Pacific cited declines. These responses indicate that in the Americas at least, some of the big productivity gains that were made in the early 1990's under pressures of falling occupancies and disappearing profits, have now been given up as revenues have soared upwards and profits have returned.

Employee Satisfaction and Performance

In view of the evident relationship between employee and customer satisfaction, our respondents were asked to rank the different approaches to improving the former. Predictably, the list was led by compensation, although our respondents anticipate this will become less important in the future. Employee recognition programs, the opportunity for career advancement and exposure to training followed in order of impact.

Improving performance is desirable but it also needs to be measured. And while most organisations tend to rely heavily on an employee's immediate supervisor for performance review, the increasing popularity of alternative systems such as self, peer and subordinate review to provide "360 degree feedback" are well worth noting as are those involving customers.

Although many would acknowledge the validity of the relationship between customer and employee satisfaction and in turn their relationship to financial performance, only 45 percent of our respondents report an integrated measurement system to account for these factors. In developing an integrated measurement system, the first step is to develop an accurate accounting of employee satisfaction. And to this end, a variety of methods are reportedly used.

The leading yardstick appears to be employee turnover - now used by 81 percent of respondents, although this should decline in the future as a greater reliance is placed on other methods. Employee surveys are destined for much greater usage in the future. And finally, upward evaluations now used by 18 percent are expected to more than double in use in the future.

2

Hotel Marketing and Sales

Given the current climate of constrained financing and reduced development plans, hotel companies are now looking at their existing operations to increase profits in the near-term. There are many ways to measure profitability for the purposes of analysing property-to-property performance. Comparisons of total profits, profits-per-available room, and of course, return-on-investment can all be employed in an effort to determine "best performers". Each method carries with it certain advantages and disadvantages. For this analysis, we have decided to compare the profitability of different hotels on a contribution margin basis. Best performers were defined as those hotels in the top 10 percent of their property category in terms of achieved profit margin.

Profits were measured after management fees, real estate taxes, and insurance, but before capital reserve, rent, interest, depreciation, amortisation, and income taxes. Like the other methods, measuring performance by comparing profit margins has its drawbacks, the first of which is the age-old argument that, "you can't take percentages to the bank." However, the ability of management to drop as many dollars to the bottom-line as possible is clearly a meaningful measure of performance.

However, the conventional belief that food and beverage service is an absolute necessity has been challenged and frequently proven to the contrary. Properties have either leased out their outlets or reduced their level of food and beverage service, while still maintaining high occupancies and rate premiums. In fact, the top performing full-service hotels all had minimal food and beverage revenue. The message is not to automatically eliminate food and beverage from your hotel. Instead, developers and managers should thoroughly exhaust all the implications of varying degrees of food and beverage service on property performance and profits.

Across the board, the average size of the top performers was consistently smaller than the average property profile for each category studied. Be it the ability to manage a smaller operation, or reach economies of scale at a lower threshold, smaller properties do appear to operate more efficiently. As might not be expected, the hotels achieving the highest profit margin in each category achieved total revenues (measured on a per available room basis) less than the average for all hotels. While the lack of food and beverage revenue would explain this occurrence for full-service hotels, it can not be the reason for limited-service properties and several all-suite properties.

To be profitable, any business must also watch their overhead expenses. Frequently, these expenses do not directly contribute to the generation of revenue for the business, and therefore, are difficult to measure in terms of payback. In the hotel industry, administrative and general expenses cover such costs as the salary and wages for the general and manager and their staff, accounting fees, security costs, credit card commissions, and human resources.

Across the board, the top performing hotels in all categories were able to control their administrative and general expenses. Measured as both a percentage of revenue and on a dollar-per-available room basis, the top performers achieved administrative and general expense margins well below the overall averages. Marketing expenses are also classified as an undistributed item. But most managers would gladly spend more, rather than less, on marketing. Once again, the achievements of the top performers appear to be counterintuitive.

Marketing expenditures by the top performers, measured as a percent of revenue, were all less than the overall averages for all property types. Even when measured on a dollar-per-available room basis, marketing expenditures for the top performing full-service and limited-service properties were short of the overall average expenditures. Apparently, the top performers were more efficient in the marketing of their properties.

What brings success to any individual hotel is a wide variety of controllable and uncontrollable factors. Some are internal, while others are external. And return-on-investment is the ultimate measure of success, and control on the investment side is just as critical as any operational techniques. The lessons to be learned from this analysis is that hotel operators need to challenge conventional wisdom.

Sales Departments

In Internet, there are lot of oppertunities for marketing. There are a variety of issues that affect the functionality of these processes online. Many of the tools are inexpensive and easy to accomplish—we need to expand the notion of how we conduct sales to include online tools as standard operational processes.

New Business Development: There are a variety of online resources available to the sales department, many by market segment. The sales department needs to be working these with the same intensity that they work trace files. If your sales department isn't making these a vital component of their prospecting activity, you can be sure that other hotels are—and gaining market share from these sites.

Pre-Approach Qualifying: There is so much information on the web—at the click of a mouse. The sales staff should be accessing information about their prospects prior to contact so that they know if they are worth pursuing. They need to know which factors to look for in reports that indicate the potential of a prospect to produce and to make a judgment about those in which they should be investing their time.

Using E-Postcards: E-postcards can be created quickly and effectively at a desktop PC. Their uses span individual prospect approaches to creating targeted e-blasts that fly under the radar of spamming. A little creativity and basic computer skills are all that are required.

E-flyers: These range from the extremely clever to the purely informative. They make an excellent vehicle for customer relationship management and to inform a broad range of guests and clients, who have given permission to receive them, of changes at the hotel and special promotions.

E-stationary: Make your hotel's email correspondence from all departments stand apart from the rest of the hotel e-chatter that hits your clients' Inbox! This can be designed to have the same look and feel as the web site and online brochures.

E-brochures: While printed brochures are not quite yet dinosaurs, how many do you have left in your hotel supply closet from the 50,000 that you ordered prior to the new renovation and addition of high-speed Internet access to your amenity list?

The Web Site: All too often the web site is developed without the input of sales or consideration of how it can be used as a sales tool—not just a design masterpiece. The inclusion of design elements and photography that appeals across and to many market segments makes it more functional for the generation of group leads. Franchise web sites offer the opportunity to include multiple photos but many hotels only include the exterior and maybe one other photo! The description screens are rarely edited to reflect seasonality and special packages. The reservation function is awkward at best—at worst it doesn't interface with the property management system.

Hotel Sales in a Limited Service Environment

Once upon a time not too long ago, prior to September 11, hotel sales in a limited service environment was reasonably straightforward. Until now, limited service hotels experienced a slight decrease in demand in most markets but not stunningly in relation to their full service competitors. Many limited serve hotels did not use a sales person, rather the GM, who had absolutely nothing else to do, was expected to function as the sales person as well.

In those situations where there was a sales person, it was usually someone with limited sales experience, perhaps promoted from the front desk. The most common reasons for this was the position was not very well paid and the job market was so tight that it was virtually impossible to attract someone with sales or hotel credentials at that salary. The rules have changed. The GM who never had time in the first place now has less time as many hotels have cut staff to respond to the dramatic drop in occupancy. While this may be somewhat shortsighted, it is the GM who is picking up the slack at the front desk and performing front office procedures.

There is no way that the GM has the time to contact all of the accounts and ascertain the conditions of the changes in their travel policies, their new rate sensitivity and what it would take to get what little remains of their business. In an environment where the rules have changed, the temptation on the part of owners and management companies is to hunker down—slash the staff to the bone, eliminate all sales and promotion expense and let the salaried managers pick up the difference by working additional hours.

Those hotels that have been operating a flabby organisation may benefit in the short term but it is not the strategy that will position a hotel to survive and succeed in the next six to nine months of uncertainty and potential recession. Make no mistake—there will be winners and losers in this new environment. The parameters of success for the winners won't be as grand as they were a brief twelve months ago but the penalties for the losers never change. Erosion of the asset and the ultimate penalty, foreclosure, is the consequence of short-term thinking. What then, are the steps to take to deal with the new rules of the game?

Formulate a strategy based on possible scenarios. Does anyone remember the Gulf War and the devastating impact it had on the travel industry in 1991? Those who survived positioned themselves well for the future. Resist the urge for knee-jerk reactions and take time to sit down and outline a unified strategy for the next twelve months. What will be the financial strategy, where is the demand likely to come from and how can we get it in the most cost-effective way possible? Ask someone from the corporate office to sit down with the staff and develop these strategies.

If that resource is not available to you, enlist the assistance of a knowledgeable but neutral outsider to facilitate the process. Many hotels did not adequately track where their business was coming from in the past when demand was high. Those hotels have a steeper learning curve than those who had the foresight to use the tracking capabilities in their franchise reservations systems. Do not ask the GM to perform this function—it is not going to happen!

If you have a sales person, be very specific about the direction you want them to take, the deals they can cut. If you don't have a sales person, get one or contract to a sales and marketing person who will perform this function for you in the short term, like the next six to nine months until things stabilise. The benefit of the latter option is that you incur no payroll burden and you can hire more expertise than you could afford long-term. Get in touch with your guests! Who are your guests the ones that fall into the transient or regular corporate category? These are the guests that 'fall through the cracks'—independent travelers, consultants, brokers, etc.

These are also the people who will continue to travel—it is their livelihood. Find out who they are and spoil them. Ask the front desk GSAs, they know the guests better than the GM. The GM should be in the lobby at check-in and/or chatting with the guests at breakfast at 6:30am. Upgrade the Guest Service staff! With the airline industry laying off so many customer service associates, it is an excellent time to hire people with experience and personality. It is an opportunity to eliminate those GSAs that were hired because they fogged the mirror—the ones who couldn't be bothered smiling at a guest or making eye contact.

Invest in some short-term training to upgrade the skills of the sales and customer service staff. If you can't afford to hire experience, train the staff you can afford. This is an investment you can't afford not to make. Find training that produces results tailored for your situation. It can be seminars or distance learning that does not require time away from the property or the job. The winners under the new rules will be those that resisted the urge to react with short-term thinking. The winners will be the ones who positioned themselves for the future and not just reacted to the immediate situation.

People will travel again by air and by car. Their requirements of us do not change—a good product and good service at a fair price. The limited service sector is well positioned to take advantage of this situation when the shock of the last two weeks wears off.

Challenge in Marketing

Hoteliers often harbor a retirement fantasy that when the mainstream career comes to a close, they will walk into the sunset and operate an inn or a bed and breakfast and will have gone to hotel heaven. Because of their size, small boutique properties often do not have the clout in the market to recruit and retain good line employees.

Seasonality can have the happy retired hotelier making beds, doing laundry and unstopping toilets in the off-season when he/she has had to lay off the seasonal staff. Any furloughs due to seasonality pretty well guarantee that the quality labor in the market will go to a property with the mass to offer them year round employment. Budgeting and forecasting can be a nightmare if accurate records of the previous years are not kept.

Benchmarking performance in the market is difficult due to lack of access and the expense of Smith Travel Research reports. Overhead and expenses can run high when the market dictates rate ceilings. The PMS systems available to independent hotels often lack the sophistication of those available to franchise properties. Inventory management is critical to maximise revenues in smaller properties and the available tools often reside in the manager's brain. If this scares you off then you should doing something else.

The rewards are the opportunity to create a guest experience based upon hospitality rather than efficiency, to implement customer service that makes memories rather than horror stories, to truly be in touch with guests rather than seeking to avoid them because a guest contact usually indicates a problem. Marketing an independent boutique hotel requires a certain finesse and accountability due to the restrictions of size and budgets.

As there is no franchise driven marketing programme and its accompanying contribution to occupancy by virtue of a GDS system and 800 numbers, nor is there a frequent guest programme, the marketing plan has to be developed and executed with precision accuracy to reach the potential guest with a true appreciation of a boutique hotel and the ability to pay the price for this level of service and intimacy. There are several key factors to develop a lean and targeted marketing plan for boutique hotels:

Begin by developing a client profile for each market segment by season. This should also include the F&B outlets. The profile should be developed demographically, geographically and fiscally. Only when you have a clear picture of your guest can you target both sales and marketing efforts and media placement. Sign up for the reservation and marketing systems available to independent hotels that best reach your client profiles. Track their production so you can review performance and make adjustments in your selection if necessary.

Use electronic distribution channels and manage the heck out them. Have a dynamite but easy to navigate web site that is capable of accepting reservations online. Ensure that your web master has you entered in the search engines by key words that appeal to your guest profile and pay for them to regularly refresh your web site positioning with the search engines. Use email to advantage when your site includes an email response capability.

Develop a Public Relations Plan within your marketing plan. The GM should be the point person for this so the sales person(s) can be dedicated to selling. The GM should be heavily community involved and serve on key committees where the visibility is highest for the target guest and/or can have access to and participate in the formulation of civic and tourism policies that benefit the hotel. Become a patron of a key charity that has a high profile with your potential guests.

Develop your own Customer Relationship Management programme. Collect as much information about your guest as possible. Not just the name and address but the kind of wine they had with dinner, events or attractions that they booked through the hotel or the hotel's concierge such as theatre tickets, special events or festivals and last but not least, whether they liked feather or foam pillows. The reservations department staff took all reservations by hand but we had a computer with a customer relationship management programme that was state of the art.

Develop cost effective mailing pieces targeted to past guests and potential guests that your profile for the period of time or promotion that you have developed. Back to the bottle of wine in you CRM system. If your or F&B outlet or an organisation in your community is sponsoring a wine festival, search the CRM for the information and mail your promotional piece to them.

Impact of Technology on Sales

The hospitality industry has used innovation and imagination to manipulate and maximise tech applications for everything from revenue management to customer relationship management. Why then have we not given more thought to the creative uses of technology in the hotel sales process? One answer is that while we have provided upgraded tech access to our guests, the sales department and administrative offices usually get hand-me-down hardware and sometimes are not even included in the high-speed Internet equation. The following are a few of the ways that hotel sales can use these tech tools to sell customers on the benefits of the hotel not just tell them about its features:

Virtual Tours

Virtual tours are great tools. The sales person should prepare for the site presentation in the same way that they would for a "live" site inspection. The good news is that with a virtual tour, you don't have to pre-inspect the rooms and it usually doesn't cost you lunch. In developing virtual tours on the web site, keep in mind that the average attention span of most people is relatively short. Pick the most representative digital photography for inclusion but limit your selections to those that will have the broadest appeal.

Bank of Digital Photography

The "bank" of photography was the same as those used to build the web site. However, there were also some that were not used on the site. Most of the phone calls were from potential customers who had visited the site but had questions or concerns or simply wanted to speak to a live human versus making their reservations on-line. Photography more often "sells" when it includes people using a feature of the hotel. For example, rather than simply having a photograph of the children's camp or playground, photos of children playing and having fun using these facilities sell the concept rather than just telling that the facility is there.

Recall those stock photos of a hotel restaurant where people are sitting at the table staring at each other but not actually eating or drinking or appearing to have fun. The people in those photos were like the furniture. The sales staff can use this photography in much the same way. Even if a planner has come for a "live" site, they often forget certain features. Many of them are coming to look at many hotels on the same trip.

Depending upon the number of hotels that they tour, their memory will often place the bathroom of one hotel in another hotel's guest room. An emailed photo will refresh their memory or speak to question or concern. It can be a powerful tool to reinforce their initial impression and overcome a potential objection. For other groups, it can also provide an image of a benefit that a client requires in one situation that they didn't require in a previous meeting.

Photography of your destination and area attractions can assist you in making the sale and promoting off-site activities. This is more powerful than simply referring them to the local tourist organisation's web site where they will also be exposed to other properties and perhaps rates.

Email Postcards

Sales people are always looking for creative ways to stay in touch with accounts. Email postcards can fill this requirement if kept fresh and not overused. Everyone understands by now that unsolicited mailings in the form of letters never get opened. Postcards, on the other hand, receive a glance prior to being thrown away. You at least have a shot at gaining the recipients attention. Unsolicited attachments to emails are like mailings in envelopes. Busy people trying to manage their Inboxes most often delete them prior to opening.

In addition, people are loath to open attachments that they are not expecting due to viruses. An email postcard opens automatically. The visual appears in the recipients

Inbox and is at least glanced at prior to deleting. This is an opportunity to gain the recipient's attention. Be very careful about not using this medium in a manner that could be considered "spam"—it should not be blasted to anyone who hasn't given "permission" to receive information about your hotel.

Let's differentiate between email "blasts" and approaching a potential new client. Email blasts to large number of recipients are extremely useful in informing past and potential customers about new developments or promotions at a property to those who have indicated a desire to receive them. An email postcard can be a way to approach a prospect when telephone contact has failed as it does frequently. This is a tailored communication to one person versus a mass communication to many.

Email postcard templates are available on newer versions of Microsoft Publisher 2002/deluxe Edition. They can be modified to contain your message or approach (remember to sell benefits to the prospect) and can contain a stock image or use an image from the bank of photography. Microsoft Outlook and Outlook Express have a Stationary feature that allows you to customise designs and colors for emails.

These are not to be used for email "blasts" but for customised communication to prospects and clients, especially when phone calls and regular emails get lost in the "chatter" of hotel solicitations. These postcards can set you apart from your competitors. It's a tough market out there. Sales people need creative tools to push the process forward.

Those who are able to relate to their clients in a technologically sophisticated way exemplify that the property and the sales staff are prepared to offer their clients the services required in a high-speed environment. Sales is the engine that drives revenue. Investing in tech tools and training sales people to use them enables them to sell in such an environment. By ensuring that they have access to these tools, the property's exposure is enhanced.

In the past hotel owners and management companies would buy products from technology vendors specialising in one area or another (front office, back office, reservations, food and beverage, sales and marketing and the like) and integrate these systems with varying degrees of success. The hospitality industry is thus beset by a multitude of technology applications offered by numerous hardware and software vendors. There are, for example, no fewer than 85 different property management Systems available to owners and managers of hotels offered by technology purveyors, some stable longterm providers to the industry, others much less so.

Meanwhile, most technology vendors continue to address individual parts of the industry's real needs with little regard to total system solutions. And hospitality companies tend to contribute to a fragmented marketplace quite simply by the way they purchase systems. It is often the case that a hotel company will buy a reservation system from one vendor, a property management system from another and a marketing system from yet another, depending on who makes the best products. And while there are proprietary "clusters" of related technology, the general fragmentation that has existed appears unlikely to change in the near future.

Even more importantly, the industry has failed to cooperate in the development of shared technologies. Moreover, little change in attitude has been evident during the past three or four years as the technology revolution continues to roll forward at an ever-quickening pace. And when a sound system solution is delivered to address an industry need, there is no mechanism for it to become an industry standard and thus picked up by others struggling with the same problem.

With the variety of applications for different parts of the business attended to by different vendors, it is not surprising that interface and integration are now major problem areas to be attended to. What some critics refer to as the industry's problem with closed architecture has undoubtedly cost the hospitality industry money, eroded efficiency and limited technology's benefits.

But the race to put technology to work for the industry also leads to other questions related to global marketing to consumers, as well as the expanding customer services that will ultimately include Internet access and other technology routinely placed in guest rooms. All this, of course, comes at a cost. The choices that hospitality companies make in the technology realm will have profound impact on competitiveness and return to investors. These choices are not easy. Indeed, they may be among the most complex the industry faces.

While integrating disparate systems is an important challenge for the industry, it is fortunately a somewhat easier task today than it has been in the past. Whereas previously hotel computer systems would tend to be free-standing and require modest maintenance, we are now migrating rapidly to environments that include Windows applications and network solutions in which that middle component is becoming a more significant element in the system. Integration is clearly an important step into the future, with connectivity established between individual property operations, customer information systems, data warehouses and centralised management.

The question for many hotel organisations remains how to achieve the ultimate open system that can be shared at all levels, whether it is the central reservation system, individual property management system or any other operational area. Until now, the center of the universe has been the property management system, but that era is ending as companies realise that an exclusive focus on the customer must be supported by fully-integrated customer information systems. Anyone who is arguing on behalf of a closed system in this kind of an environment is arguing against the market.

Not all the responsibility for integration, however, lies with technology providers. On the buyer's side there must be greater recognition of the commonality of needs regardless of the type of hotel property involved. Is it really necessary to continue to re-invent the wheel, for example, with all of the differing property management systems now available in the market? Even more, can the hospitality industry agree on technology standards, which are essential for full conformance and integration of systems? If the vendors can agree on interfaces between their products and other subsystems, the hospitality industry could benefit greatly.

There may be some rationale for keeping certain applications proprietary to individual companies and their properties. But falling to support development of shared interfaces between systems is short-sighted at best. And ultimately it is not the hardware or even the software that delivers the competitive advantage it lies in what management does with the information when it gets it. Note that the successful hospitality organisation of the future is one which reduces the traditional bias towards analysis with an associated increase in creativity. If the industry is to come together and buy into the development of common standards, it will require acknowledgment of this reality.

Technology Cycles

Timing is everything in technology investments. For hotel management, knowing when to invest in technology and what new developments to purchase is critical to managing the long-term cost and the benefit of investment in technology. A recent survey suggests that the hospitality industry as a whole has been more conservative than most in making technology investments. Microsoft - in concert with Lodging Magazine and Hospitality and Automation recently completed an industry-wide survey of technology applications in use and plans for the future. The survey results revealed that more than 70 percent of respondents are using property management systems word processing spreadsheet, accounting and point-of-sale applications. Fifty percent have sales and catering applications and 20 to 35 percent use presentation programs and scheduling.

The Microsoft survey further discovered that 25 to 30 percent of respondents plan to install property management systems, e-mail, sales and catering, point-of-sale and accounting systems in the next 42 months. On the basis of these results, even the biggest supporter of efforts to systematise our processes would have to acknowledge that this industry remains far behind many others. But with the recent upturn in the industry's fortunes, together with the increased availability of technology at lower per-unit costs than ever before, there are clearly plans to increase spending.

The Microsoft-sponsored survey, in fact, went on to discover that 25 to 30 percent of respondents plan to install property management, e-mail, sales and catering, point-of-sale and accounting systems in the next 42 months. Longer term (over the next five years), 60 to 70 percent plan to install property management, office automation, accounting and sales systems, while 50 percent plan on telecom and food and beverage systems. Forty percent will add in-room applications. Even with these plans, however, there is clearly much to be accomplished in bringing the industry into the next millennium - at least from a technology standpoint.

Technology breakthroughs are generally considered to be cyclical. New applications are coming to market faster than ever before, and the time between conception and implementation grows shorter. It has been said that technology development in the industry once ran in seven- to -nine year cycles. This undoubtedly is no longer the case, however. In terms of pure technology, recycling appears to be occurring virtually every other year now. For the hospitality industry, the technology development cycle probably breaks into three- to five-year intervals.

Indeed, the next breakthroughs in hospitality technology may occur when the property management system is finally dislodged from its place at the center of hotel computer systems. The next big cycle will focus on the fully integrated system that brings customer, statistical and financial information together through an integration of property management, central reservations, data warehouse and distributed database systems. This appears to be where a number of the larger chains already are heading.

Network Centric Computing

We are on the threshold of some major breakthroughs in the use of network centric computing, an expression coined by IBM to describe the remote off-site world of data collection, information processing and system application that occurs in cyberspace. The integration of computing, telecommunications and interactive cable television to move information is driving this evolution, which will eventually create a seamless bridge for global sources of information.

It is only a matter of time until the Internet evolves into a single, powerful highway of information supported by diverse technology applications, many already in development. At the same time, the hospitality industry will also benefit from the development of intranets, internal networks built with the same standards and infrastructure as the Internet and World Wide Web. Intranets today offer the potential for streamlined and enhanced internal communication, and may be particularly beneficial for large organisations with scattered operations.

Further out on the horizon is the prospect of an outsourcing vehicle that can supply the computing service to all-comers, even single hotel property owners who otherwise face a distinct competitive disadvantage as the technology revolution passes them by. And lest the particularly demanding hotel chain be concerned about its unique needs, there should also be the opportunity within an outsourced networked system for appropriate customisation at reasonable cost.

Network computing has enormous implications for marketing to customers on a global basis, as well as hotel operations. Consider the potential for the industry to connect with vendors worldwide for electronic purchasing, potentially achieving economies of scale and leveraging not yet possible. World purchasing functions will allow companies to customise their own catalogs.

Virtual channels of distribution using computer networking capabilities will also allow hotel companies to market products and services - some traditional to our industry, others not - to customers whether they are in the hotel, at work, or at home. This will require a migration from today's central reservation systems to tomorrow's customer information systems using network-centric solutions. Development of customer profiles and guest recognition will make it possible for hotel organisations to interact in entirely new ways with customers, regardless of their physical location.

Clearly, the large hotel companies will need to be the first to address questions raised by global networking capabilities and what this will mean in terms of technology investment. But for many hospitality companies presently struggling with the high cost of technology and the confusing state of our industry's technology affairs, this will not be an easy task. And the decisions will ultimately become further complicated by the opportunity to outsource certain functions into subscription-based networks.

It is unlikely that the hospitality industry will be forced to bear the entire burden for networking infrastructure. Strategic alliances with major technology companies will be the catalysts in building this capability as they become strategic providers of networking capabilities to hospitality and other industries. And as network-centric computing comes of age and a company's proprietary information is stored in cyberspace, security will become an ever-more important issue requiring solutions. Whether it is an e-mail gateway through an internal network or customer access via the Internet, network fire walls and encryption systems will be required to mitigate the concern many will have with system security.

In the final analysis, networking solutions will drive down the cost of technology investment "on-property" where hotel real estate and business interests merge. The solutions that hotel organisations will be able to choose from in terms of networking should also be less expensive than the current profile of technology spending. And we can expect that change to occur sooner rather than later, given the present rate of investment in Internet-based technologies.

Role of Internet

The Internet is having a huge impact on how we conduct our lives and our businesses. And it arrived virtually overnight. In the United States, for example, it took 38 years for television to get into 50 million homes. For the

Internet, it took just five years. And for those U.S. consumers that are online, four out of five believe that the Internet is a more important invention than television. Of these same online consumers, close to six in 10 prefer e-mail to paper mail for business correspondence and over one in four check their e-mail while on vacation.

The Internet is also changing the customer relationship—undermining and redirecting customer attention to new sellers of products and services and away from their traditional relationships. And as this occurs, the traditional approaches that hospitality businesses have taken to distribution are all being affected. From reservations taken over the Internet, which are projected to more than double to 9% of volume over the next year, to the declining role of the travel agent. This occurs as so-called "infomediaries" provide information and access, and software robots troll the activity online to develop matches between buyers and sellers, analysing complex patterns and looking for trends for marketers to capitalise upon. As for the infomediaries, we can expect some of these to move into the transactions business and continue the process of disintermediation. For some hospitality companies, it may be best to join this new competition, particularly if it cannot be beaten at its own game.

The reality today is that the balance of power is shifting from sellers to buyers and in so doing it makes the importance of delivering high-quality service, convenience and value for money ever more compelling. The Internet has clearly leveled the playing field by making price information broadly available to the consumer. Internet business models affect product and services offerings, pricing, distribution and customer service, as well as long-term information capabilities. As a consequence, some hospitality suppliers will inevitably feed different tranches of their inventory through the various channels at their disposal—including the Internet, travel management organisations, destination packagers and the like.

In the end, customers want both convenience and consistency. They don't have all the leisure time that futurists once predicted they would have by now. In fact, they have less. Today's fast-paced world produces ever more stress, and consumers want information and they want it fast. And if hospitality companies and travel providers don't deliver convenience, somebody else inevitably will. They also want to be wired up to the rest of the world—at home, in their office and especially when they travel. And for hoteliers trying to cope with in-room technologies and the delivery of high-speed Internet access, we will soon be seeing more integration of network communication and entertainment products to further complicate or liberate our lives, depending on your point of view. Customers are also looking for consistency—a simple concept, but central to whether a brand has value or not. And in the emerging networked world, aligning the value propositions of alliance partners and ensuring a seamless and consistent experience will only be as good as the weakest link in the chain.

Hospitality E-business

E-business is rewriting the economic rules globally for every industry—including hospitality, travel and leisure. Indeed, it's important to recognise that we are now operating in what has been described as the "new economy," as global trends drive change, including globalisation, consolidation, convergence, technology and communications. Even more, it is clear that the underlying sources of value are also changing. Use of intangible assets such as information, brands, customers, relationships and networks distinguish the most successful companies in the world.

In some industries, profits are made on spare parts and maintenance rather than on mainstream products. In the new economy, we may see this business model replicated in the hospitality industry. And for those companies that discount or give away products such as hotel rooms in order to sell linked services, they surely will be redefining the meaning of hospitality. They will also be marketing an array of hospitality and leisure products and services to a customer base that is no longer satisfied with the traditional ways of making such purchases.

Hospitality businesses that traditionally provided room, board, management and marketing may need to rethink their roles in the new economy, particularly as services become more valuable than products. With the rapid growth of "infomediaries" and their facilitation of transactions, hospitality businesses may need to redefine themselves in order to prosper in an increasingly electronic world where one-to-one customisation is the order of the day. But for those contemplating repositioning their companies in an e-business environment, it will be necessary to focus on the current value proposition of the business and determine how it might be reformatted or enhanced to ensure success in the new setting.

As information technology (IT) is used to facilitate a company's entry into the world of electronic commerce, our industry's leadership will also need to overcome a natural tendency to be disappointed by the role of IT in achieving competitive advantage. For many years IT was seen as a mechanism to support back office finance and accounting functions. In the future, it inevitably will be one of the principal drivers of value creation in the new economy. But we should not be mislead by IT—in e-business, it will be the strategy, not the technology that will make the difference between success and failure. But having the strategy in place is only the first step. It must be linked to every part of the business.

With the costs of playing in the e-business world escalating rapidly, hospitality executives should consider the four phases of what might be called the "E-Business Lifecycle." The first of these—E-Business Strategy Development and Planning—must address the market and competitive context, articulate the vision and opportunity, outline the strategy and the business case, and identify the risks. In recent years, we have frequently seen hospitality businesses put up a Web site on the Internet and consider this an e-business strategy. But without a strategy for this new form of commerce and the business planning process to drive it, such reactionary approaches stand little chance for success.

Once the plan is in place, an e-business design phase can commence to address site design, lay out the business architecture, identify the technical infrastructure, plan for performance, availability and capacity, and deal with tax issues and enterprise security. Following the design phase, E-Business implementation will prepare for the launch with training and change enablement, implementation and integration, testing and roll-out. Once in place, E-Business Operations will need to be supported by IT and audit services, Web site activity analysis and Web site maintenance. Finally, measurement systems will need to be established to monitor performance.

As industry executives embark on this e-business lifecycle, they will need in the first stage to clearly establish the business case for investing in new technologies, systems and organisations by addressing both the cost reduction and revenue enhancement benefits. On the revenue side, there are a number of factors to consider. These include the company's ability to identify and recruit the most valuable customers; the ability to seamlessly cross-sell the company's products and services, as well as those of alliance partners; the ability to retain valuable customers and reduce attrition; and finally, when and how to eliminate costly and unnecessary discounts through revenue optimisation.

In this kind of environment, the property management system will no longer hold sway as the center of the hospitality universe, but will become just one in a series of customer touch-points that will increasingly include the Internet. These touch-points will ultimately need to be fully integrated into a customer information system supported by sophisticated data warehousing and data mining technologies.

Adding to the industry's costs in this portrait of the future is the cost of grafting e-business technologies onto the industry's legacy systems. At a certain stage, it may make sense to start from scratch and ensure that every system is Web-enabled. This would allow a total interface for a high-growth e-business, thereby maximising the customer relationship management opportunities that it presents.

As to the role of the Internet, its comprehensive reach and ubiquitous nature has already ensured its central place in the new economy. But how should we evaluate whether an Internet application is deserving of our attention? Firstly, productivity on the Internet in the years to come will be vastly improved by much higher bandwidth than is currently in place. And with higher bandwidth will come applications that can benefit from such extra capacity delivering tightly focused and reliable content to an increasingly sophisticated and demanding e-customer. If an Internet application is to succeed in the future, it will therefore need to be designed to capitalise on this coming reality.

Secondly, an Internet application needs to form a community of some sort because without a sense of place, albeit of the virtual sort participants will not have that all-important sense of belonging. And as with the industrial revolution, which drew a disparate population to centers of economic activity, so will such "intranet communities" grow in value as their populations increase in size and their economic product expands. For larger businesses that form such communities, they are developing new revenue sources and are reinventing their relationships with customers, employees, suppliers and partners. Smaller companies intent on participating in this new environment, may need to be content as a participant in an established community, rather than trying to take on the creation of a community itself. It is better, perhaps, to be one of many players in a successful space than struggling to establish an identity in a world surrounded by also-rans.

Whether large or small, community developers and marketers of the virtual sort will have to recognise that what may have appeared cool in the physical world to generations brought up in the old economy will not work in the world of e-business. Being cool and staying that way in order to get and keep attention will remain a constant challenge, especially for those keen to nurture a younger generation of travelers brought up on MTV and the Web.

Finally, the successful Internet application needs to improve service while reducing transaction costs, particularly as the balance of power in the buy/sell relationship continues its inexorable migration from sellers to buyers. Service improvement strategies will be nothing new for hospitality businesses, but it is noteworthy that service is the top factor that encourages return e-business. This must be an area of focus since the current growth of e-business appears destined to outpace the supporting infrastructure and its related service at least over the short term. But as hospitality executives know, delivering good service can be expensive.

Scaling the types of service response to the circumstances is a growing need, but one that can be modulated if the value of each customer can be distinguished and the response adjusted accordingly. In considering the opportunities in hospitality e-business, industry leaders should take stock of the dynamics that are occurring in the new economy and plan accordingly. It is probably easy to dismiss the e-business world as a playground for others with products and services that are more obviously applicable. But our industry is changing, as is the world around us.

Client Server Technology

The technology life cycle provides a model to assess how and when companies and individuals adopt new technologies. Pioneers are generally the first to acquire new technologies and take the greatest risk. A second category of technology users—leaders—adopt relatively unproven technologies, but the risks are known and accepted. Obsolete technology at the other end of the spectrum may seriously impair a company's ability to compete. In terms of costs and benefits, the best balance appears to be with the leaders who invest significantly less than pioneers and incur reduced risks, yet their technology investments can yield similar benefits.

Finding that balance in technology investment is critical today for hotel operations, given its importance in two areas:

— The desire of operators to improve the guest experience. This is demonstrated through faster check-in and check-out, more timely response to service requests and a myriad of other opportunities to enhance services.

— The potential to improve operating efficiencies. Hotel operators are seeking ways to reduce staffing requirements, cross-train staff, reduce the overall general and administrative expense, and explore opportunities for centralising some functions while at the same time distributing other functions more widely.

Implementing technological advances promises the potential for greatly enhanced guest services to meet rising customer expectations, improved cost control, more effective marketing strategies and expanded opportunities for hotel companies and properties to achieve a competitive advantage. However, technology is only as good as its application by an organisation, and therein lies the challenge for hospitality companies‹ weighing how best to invest in technology, as well as train employees and implement its use.

A retrospective view of how high technology has been used in the hospitality industry reveals the depth of change wrought in hotel operations during the past four decades. Accounting and financial systems were introduced during the 1960s, but exclusively as mainframe-based systems operated by the largest hotels. Systems oriented to property management were introduced in the 1970s. During the 1980s, systems were ported to mini-computer and micro-computer based platforms. Accounting, financial and property management systems finally became available even to the smallest operators. Sales and marketing applications were developed to provide a competitive advantage for properties.

The 1990s will be marked as the decade of integration, driven by powerful networking capabilities offered by client server technology. This technology will bring no less than the dismantling of the management information system (MIS) paradigm as we have known it, more completely democratising access to information than at any time in the past.

Client server computing currently has no standard, agreed-upon definition. Generally, however, the client server architecture involves integrated, networked computer systems using applications cooperating across the network, according to Stewart Alsop of InfoWorld. Instead of having a series of mainframes networked together, client server architectures involve one large processor unit and a network of clients linked together, often across large geographic areas. Client server systems make the best use of both the networked client computers processing and user interface abilities, and the server systems database, computational and data management abilities.

Client server architectures offer major benefits to companies adopting these systems. Data access is faster because the server is not burdened with running applications. Data access is more evenly distributed, and users have the ability to query and create their own reports. At the same time, design of the database can be truly independent of the applications, which are run on the user computers.

Client server technology in the hospitality industry offers significant opportunities as companies make decisions relating to technology. In addition to improving services, hotel operators are seeking ways to effectively integrate the disparate systems accumulated during the last decade. Most of the larger hotel properties currently are running multiple computer platforms, and due to the cost of technology, will continue to do so for the next several years. These platforms have evolved from a patchwork of tactical solutions initiated by various functional areas.

Client server technology is probably the most viable strategic option for medium to large multi-property owners and operators as technology upgrades are made. The number of enterprises in general industry that have adopted client server architectures, for example, has risen from 35 percent in 1992 to more than 60 percent today, according to the research firm, International Data Corporation. Similar levels of use can be expected in the hospitality industry.

Client server technology benefits hotel organisations primarily because it decouples the applications from the database contained on the "server"system. In practical terms, this means that the applications typically used in the hospitality industry can be developed by different vendors, yet use a common database. Ad hoc reporting and MIS support are simplified and more efficient.

The client server approach, then, makes it possible to rebuild an information technology (IT) infrastructure to unify mainframes, midrange systems and PCs with universal connectivity in a single infrastructure as the ultimate goal. Optimally, hotel organisations should be able to reduce IT costs, leverage investments in PCs and improve staff productivity. In addition, client server technology sets the stage for the still more sophisticated technologies of the next decade in which guests will have greater access to in-room technologies, and fully integrated systems using a common database will be the norm.

Advantages of New Technologies

Customer Savvy

Today, the hospitality industry's customers - hotel guests at large -have become increasingly dependent on technology - and more demanding in terms of in-room technology support. This is particularly true for the business traveler whose laptop computer often serves as a mobile office. Technology-driven entertainment options for guests - both business and leisure - also will require investments in the future. Indeed, Internet access will likely be a routine guest service at some point for hotel organisations seeking to remain competitive. And it is hoped we will find inexpensive reengineering solutions that will allow technology to be introduced into physical spaces (such as hotel rooms) without necessitating huge expenditures on rewiring and retooling of existing equipment. The signs of late are encouraging.

Both IBM and Oracle are working on low-end PC products that will provide all of the relevant network interfaces and windowing required. With prices expected in the range of $300 to $700 per device, these appliances will serve an exclusive networking function for economical use in the home. And there are more such products to come as other major technology companies go to market with similar offerings. Clearly, such devices have implications for use in hotel guest rooms. The industry has historically "mortgaged" its guest room space to third-party providers of entertainment service. In this coming wave of in-room technology, there may be an opportunity for hotel companies to become more proactive in the development and provision of in-room communications and networking solutions that will inevitably need to be provided in the hotel product of the future.

As technology evolves in our industry, we can expect customers to do more and more for themselves. This is already the case with lobby check-in kiosks and use of the Internet as an electronic travel agent to book hotel rooms. Indeed, those capabilities call into question the future of travel agents. What role will travel agents play in the face of increasingly direct customer access to the industry's reservation systems? If your title has the word "agent" in it, it is probably time to be concerned about the tightening of the direct relationship between hospitality companies and their customers, which is now being facilitated by technology.

Ultimately, customers may use Web casting devices that will allow them to create the best itinerary for travel based on a custom-designed profile. The workforce has become increasingly mobile as people work at home and from hotel rooms all over the world. In the future, it is likely that travel related companies will provide booking software modules for use by large corporate customers and individuals alike that will work on home or office computers - with customised profile information that includes hotel and airline preferences or restrictions set by company travel policies. Such a trend will increase the pressure on hospitality companies to respond with sophisticated yield management systems and marketing approaches.

Yield Management

Yield management - often today referred to as revenue optimisation has come to the hospitality industry via the airline business where high-tech solutions to forecasting based on complex algorithms have generated tremendous improvements in yield. But for yield management to become truly effective in the hospitality industry, much more will need to be accomplished in terms of technology support and the interface between the market reality at the property level and the centralised reservations Systems that have now become such an important part of the industry's distribution system.

Consider what the industry was like before automation. All of the room inventory existed at the individual property level. Over the course of time, hotel companies fractionalised that inventory. Some remained at the property, while other parts moved to a central inventory or out to a global distribution system. Of the various challenges facing hospitality companies in the future, the task of bringing that inventory back to a central location is a significant one. Such an inventory would produce a single image that can be accessed by all points in the distribution system and would generate consistent information as to availability and pricing - a simple concept with tangible benefits but one that has yet to penetrate this industry. With revenue enhancement opportunities variously estimated in the five- to seven-percent range as such systems are centralised, this should be a quick win for our industry.

Telecommunications

The current state of telecommunications is confusing to most business people in those countries that are privatising and deregulating their telecom industries, In these countries, we can thus assume that the hospitality industry is in a similar state. The telecom business is in a state of flux worldwide and with deregulation, we can expect more options and competitive pricing. In the United States, for example, it is conceivable that hoteliers will eventually be able to look to one vendor for all telcom needs - local, long distance, 800 number services, cellular, in-room entertainment, data services and Internet access.

Voice activation systems will soon arrive in central reservations offices, announcing the beginning of the early breakthroughs in the linking of computing and telecommunications. And as the telecom business continues to privatise and deregulate, the battle for customers will escalate. Clearly, the industry's leadership will need to keep an eye on this. It will probably take a while for all the dust to settle especially in the United States where there appears to be a free-for-all in this arena. But the end result should be lower unit pricing - an essential element for the hospitality industry as it seeks to align a seamless integration of the telecom and computer systems sides of its business. For international hospitality companies with chains of properties in countries around the world, the outlook should be more circumspect. For such enterprises the delivery of consistent basic telephone service in some countries will clearly need to precede further advancement of telecom technology.

3

Destination Marketing Strategy

Destination Promotion

Promotion is an important part of any tourism programme. For ecotourism and nature-based tourism programmes, certain factors need to be considered before any promotion begins. Specifically, the fragility of the sites that tourists will be visiting, the impacts that visitor use will have on the area, and the level of visitation that can be sustained without harming the area need to be identified. For example, areas hig'hly impacted by even a small degree of visitor use should either be not promoted at all or promoted to an extremely limited degree. Word-of-mouth advertising often attracts enough visitors to these areas already, making additional promotion unnecessary. Areas that can handle a larger number of visitors without being negatively impacted can be promoted to a greater extent.

Certain types of tourism fit a site's goals and objectives better than others. As with any management action, promotional campaigns should reflect the site's stated policy vision statement and objectives. For example, at natural sites, if local economic development is an objective, managers may wish to promote bird-watching or trekking where local people may be hired as guides or drivers. At an archaeological site affected by theft of objects destined for trafficking in stolen art, a promotional programme may be designed to attract better-off visitors who are willing to pay an extra fee to support an artisan cooperative making high-quality replicas of objects at the site. These can then be sold to satisfy a portion of the demand fed by trafficking.

The segmentation process requires research into the characteristics and preferences of visitors who may want to come to a site. Distinct segments of consumers might include those belonging to museum associations or organisations for the protection of wildlife. Identifying people with similar motivations and needs enables the manager to pinpoint the types of promotional materials needed. A simple example is an elderly target audience, for whom promotional materials can be in larger print and may list special services for senior citizens.

To be selected for management action, a market segment must have three characteristics:

— it must be measurable,

— it should be easy to reach through promotional distribution systems, and

— it should promise increased earnings sufficient to more than repay the costs of targeting it with promotional materials.

Knowing how tourists inform themselves on a site they wish to visit will help identify where to focus promotional efforts: For example, since most "eco-tourists" wishing to see polar bears in Manitoba, Canada, seek information from travel agents, the site's managers are wise to send their promotional materials to travel agencies. However, since few travel agencies are able or willing to stock the full range of available brochures and are ill-prepared to deal with specialised inquiries, a more efficient approach may be to send agents a brochure and then contact them personally to brief them on the site's attractions and the logistics of reaching it.

Developing a theme using a site's central message for the park's promotion helps develop marketing and promotional materials. Combining a site's most attractive elements to develop slogans or "soundbites", will facilitate the design and creation of brochures and interpretation displays. For instance, a park could be "the best kept secret in the Caribbean", or the place where "billions of years of nature meet thousands of years of history".

An analysis of strengths, weaknesses, opportunities and threats (SWOT) can be used to identify gaps between a site's promotion strategy and tourism trends. A SWOT analysis is a marketing tool used to evaluate a site's promotional abilities by examining the strengths and weaknesses of its promotional organisation, financial and staff resources, and existing promotional strategy. Strengths and weaknesses are considered factors over which the site has some control; opportunities and threats are external. Strengths and weaknesses include:

— the ways in which the site is being marketed, the size of the marketing budget, performance measures and the degree and nature of the staff's involvement in marketing efforts

— the site's tourism products, including the quality of service, image and reputation

— a profile of current visitors

— suppliers and the quality of goods and services they provide

— the people who handle any marketing for the site and the image they promote, for example, the way it is presented by tour operators compared with the site's own promotional materials.

— political factors, including government legislation

— economic factors

— social factors
— competition, identifying competitors and analysing their strengths and weaknesses

Managers without sufficient time or staff to carry out promotional tasks may consider seeking outside assistance. Tasks such as writing to guidebook publishers, magazines and newspapers to publicise attractions and present management issues are time-consuming and vie for a manager's attention. An independent promotional organisation representing the different interest groups may provide a solution. Such a group can analyse a site's tourism market and management realities. It has the further virtue of being independent, so that it can bridge gaps between competing interest groups.

A group such as an NGO with ties to the site and that knows the tourism business, or a government group with a mandate to coordinate all the stakeholders could play this role. An independent organisation set up to facilitate tourism and park promotion at Lake Baikal, Russia, produced a guidebook giving the names of local tour operators and guides, and distributed it in North America, Europe and Japan. If an outside organisation is solicited, it must be given clear direction so that its output reflects the site's goals and objectives. For example, if a goal is to support local entrepreneurs, such as ground operators, the organisation must ensure that it promotes both smaller local operators as well as larger or regional and national companies.

Developing a site's "tourism identity" is an essential element of a promotional strategy. This identity, which is based on the site's goals, objectives and market potential, becomes associated with the site in the minds of potential visitors. It could centre on a famous fresco or an endangered animal, for example, and be used to develop a logo for future promotional activities.

Site Promotion Strategies

International tourist guidebooks can be a free source of promotion. Guidebooks are a popular source of information for trip planning and are available for almost every country and region of the world. Because guidebook information is constantly changing, new editions are regularly updated, and editors are usually willing to publish information free of charge. This presents an opportunity to have information on a site and local attractions and services distributed to a wide audience.

Supplying information to travel magazines, newspapers, radio and the internet is another costeffective way to promote a site. Travel magazines and newspapers publish information on tourism attractions free of charge and local radio and television stations broadcast such information as a public service. These can all be useful sources of free publicity for the site. In-flight airline magazines reach a large public, and because they are published quarterly or bimonthly, articles remain in circulation for considerable periods. Most publications can be accessed by the internet and the information transferred in this manner.

Brochures can be used to distribute site information to a wide range of audiences. They can be mailed to national tourism offices, included in promotional information sent to tour operators, newspapers, magazines, radio and television stations and distributed to hotels. However, unlike other types of promotional material, brochures are costly to produce, and should be designed to remain valid over a long period of time. Most people who receive brochures read them. However, research has found that brochures are likely to exert more influence on people who have not visited a site before and less likely to attract repeat visitors.

Contacting tour operators directly is a useful means of interesting them in a site. Tour operators are always on the lookout for new attractions to sell to their clients. Operators, particularly companies that specialise in activities offered at the site, will appreciate receiving a brochure and any information about the local community. Direct contact with tour operators bypasses travel agencies and improves the chances of a positive response.

Producing an information package to area attractions and services can help direct benefits to local residents. If one of the goals of a site's tourism programme is to benefit local communities, a multi-lingual community guide sheet may be a valuable promotional tool. It can direct visitors to neighbouring destinations and attractions, providing a detailed picture of what the area offers, including dining, shopping and accommodations. The information is especially useful for attracting the independent traveller. Such a package should be distributed to key points such as hotels in major cities and at national tourism offices or embassies abroad. If a site has internet, it can be distributed electronically. A guide can also be used as a management tool for bringing about desired visitor behaviour, by for example discussing cultural rules and taboos and good conservation practices. Such a guide can be produced by the community with the help of site management. A local NGO may provide free computer time and translating services. Selling the guide even if it is very simple may help pay for future copying expenses.

National tourism offices or embassies can be a free and effective means of distributing promotional materials. Tour operators are always on the lookout for new attractions to sell to their clients. Operators, particularly companies that specialise in activities offered at the site, will appreciate receiving a brochure and any information about the local community. Direct contact with tour operators bypasses travel agencies and improves the chances of a positive response.

Holding a press day can be an effective way to introduce a site to the media. The day can be scheduled to coincide with a cultural celebration at the site, or it could be a yearly event held to mark the beginning of the tourist season. Tour operators, hotel owners and government officials who belong to the site's advisory group can be recruited to play a role. These stakeholders usually have press contacts and may be interested in obtaining media coverage of their activities or businesses. National tourist offices sometimes organise familiarisation tours for travel writers whose expenses paid by the government or large tourist enterprises. To get a site included on a familiarisation tour is not easy, but the manager may approach the tourism ministry or perhaps a hotel chain with promotional materials.

If no outside funding is available stakeholders may be able to offer or raise financial support. If foreign press are invited, local business people are more likely to contribute time and resources to the event. Familiarisation visits for the international media are most successful if the journalists invited have special interests that match the activities of a site, such as the theatre or marine protection. One method of identifying appropriate journalists is to find their by-lines in the international press.

Tourism Promotion in Protected Areas

Tourism activities in and around protected areas can have both positive and negative impacts on local people and the environment. Tourism can benefit a national park or other protected area by serving as a financing mechanism, with direct revenues from user fees and taxes used to protect biological resources and maintain natural areas. Intangible benefits can include increased awareness of and support for the purpose and role of protected areas, by both local communities and tourists. If tourism is important to the local or national economy, it may encourage authorities to manage and maintain protected areas more effectively, benefiting tourists, local communities and the environment. The negative environmental impacts of tourism can include water and soil contamination from construction or improper disposal of solid waste and wastewater, air pollution from transportation, wildlife habitat destruction, and land degradation.

Successfully addressing the challenges of tourism in protected areas requires strong co-operation among all parties, including those operating within and outside protected area boundaries, as well as those that can promote effective management of protected areas by ensuring that the appropriate planning and management tools are adopted. Although the goals of different stakeholders can be quite varied, tourism activities can only be sustainable if implemented with a common understanding and consensus-based approach to development.

Tour operators play a central role in the tourism industry. As intermediaries between tourists and tourism service suppliers, tour operators can influence the choices of consumers, the practices of suppliers and the development patterns of destinations. This unique role means that tour operators can make an important contribution to furthering the goals of sustainable tourism development and protecting the environmental and cultural resources on which the tourism industry depends for its survival and growth. The members of the Tour Operators' Initiative believe that tourism in protected areas should be:

— Developed and implemented with the consensus of, and in close co-operation with, relevant stakeholders;

— Supported by effective policies, guidelines, management strategies and technical tools; and o

Focused on conserving the environment while ensuring economically, socially and culturally sound development.

The members of the Tour Operators' Initiative also believe that tour operators can contribute to the sustainable development of tourism in protected areas in many different ways, such as:

— Including protected areas in their itineraries and giving customers information about the natural and cultural features of visited sites and their roles in the conservation of local ecosystems;

— Limiting the size of their groups, or dividing large groups into smaller ones when visiting protected areas;

— Informing protected area managers of visits ahead of time and discussing ways to reduce visitor impacts;

— Integrating sustainability principles into the selection criteria and service agreements of their suppliers, and choosing locally owned and operated suppliers;

— Making financial contributions to conservation and development projects;

— Providing customers with opportunities to proactively support protected areas; and

— Providing customers with guidelines on how to avoid negative impacts while visiting sensitive areas, for example by maintaining appropriate distances from wildlife, staying on trails to avoid trampling plants or causing erosion, and keeping water and energy use down to avoid related impacts on the environment.

Discovery Initiatives (UK) offers Discoverer Holidays, which allow customers to get involved as field assistants in specific research projects. For example, a tour in Kalimantan, Indonesia, on the island of Borneo, allows travellers to work with the world's leading orang-utan study programme and contributes US$1,000 per client to the Orang-utan Foundation in Tanjing Putung National Park. Dynamic Tours (Morocco) has developed a Mountain and Desert Guide's Charter for its guides, as a means to build awareness on their roles as liaisons to travellers on:

— Environmental problems;

— Economic impacts of groups in a given area;

— Financial resources generated by tourism and their role in preserving local species and heritage;

— Local social and economic development; and

— Appropriate and sustainable environmental and social practices.

Exodus (UK) has a Responsible Tourism policy that includes:

— Hiring more local guides to provide better experiences and support to local communities;

— Purchasing local products and services, where appropriate, for all trips;

— Working with local operators to implement the policy; and

— Limiting group size based on local situations.

Hapag-Lloyd Kreuzfahrten (Germany) specialises in expedition and luxury river and ocean cruises, particularly in the Arctic, Antarctica, the South Pacific Islands and the Amazon basin. To minimise the environmental impacts of its tours and improve the experience of its customers, the company has developed a handbook for travellers to Antarctica, which provides:

— Guidelines and practical information for appropriate behaviour in Antarctica;

— Historical, geological and scientific facts to accompany lectures offered on cruises; and

— Supplementary reading on Antarctica, covering topics such as the region's history, the Antarctic Treaty, native plants and animals, and environmental issues in the region.

Hotelplan (Switzerland) established an Eco-Fund in January 2001. Funds are raised through a contribution of five Swiss Francs (about US$3) per customer on any of Hotelplan's 'Holidays at the Seaside' packages, which represent 20-25 percent of sales. In 2002, the fund raised about US$750,000. The money is used for internal and external sustainable tourism projects, environmental efforts by partners at Hotelplan destinations, and emergency help in case of natural disasters or one-off projects.

Premier Tours (US), which specialises in safari tours to Southern and East Africa, selects tented camps and lodges in national parks and private game reserves that are committed to sustainable practices and apply a sensible approach to tourism, conservation and local community involvement. Premier Tours favours camps that:

— Employ full-time ecologists to ensure sustainable environmental practices in camps;

— Provide electricity through solar panels;

— Do not allow hunting, but support photographic safaris;

— Provide for direct or indirect benefits to local communities and/or conservation projects;

— Have garbage removed to appropriate places for safe disposal; and

— Have lined tanks for safe sewage processing.

TUI Nederland (the Netherlands) launched the Environmentally Aware Tourism project in Bonaire and Curaçao in 1999, to provide customers with information on responsible travel and sustainable products. Initial information is provided in the brochures of TUI

Nederland's brands Arke and Holland International. Once a client has chosen a holiday to Bonaire or Curaçao:

— TUI Nederland provides tips for environmentally sound practices in the voucher booklet that includes their air tickets;

— KLM, a project partner, shows an on-board video about the sustainable excursions and activities that are part of the project;

— Upon arrival, trained TUI Nederland hostesses introduce guests to the sustainable excursions and activities that are available; and

— The TUI Nederland resource book, available in hotel lobbies, further directs guests to sustainable excursions, activities and attractions.

Viaggi del Ventaglio (Italy) decided in 1998 to grant US$1 per bed/night to the Ministry of Tourism of the Dominican Republic, to help repair damage from Hurricane George. Contributions lasted for one year and generated about US$150,000. Part of the funds were invested in the conservation and development of Saona Island, inside the Parque Nacional del Este.

The island represents a unique and beautiful, but delicate, ecosystem, and is a favourite excursion for hotels located in the area. Funds were also used to reconstruct 63 houses in the village of Manojuan, which was badly damaged by the hurricane, and to promote and develop local handicrafts, through grants to local enterprises.

Role of Tour operators

Tour operators is the most important factor in the tourism industry. As intermediaries between tourists and tourism service suppliers, tour operators can make an important contribution to furthering the goals of sustainable tourism development and protecting the environmental and cultural resources on which the tourism industry depends for its survival and growth. It is thus in the tour operators' interest to preserve the environment in destinations and establish good relationships with local communities, to improve the quality of their tourism products and increase customer satisfaction. The members of the Tour Operators' Initiative for Sustainable Tourism Development (TOI) recognise that they cannot achieve their sustainability goals without working in partnership with all stakeholders in the destinations where they operate.

TOI members have committed to establish and strengthen links and develop partnerships with local authorities, the private sector, civil society and non-governmental organisations (NGOs) in the destinations they visit. The TOI's network offers its members the opportunity to approach them together, with a common voice, and develop in a full participatory approach a shared vision on sustainable development and a common action plan, which is the base for a solid partnership between tour operators and the various destination stakeholders.

Side, on the southern coast of Turkey, is the first destination in which the TOI members have forged a partnership with the local stakeholders. TOI members and their local partners bring to Side approximately 300,000 tourists each year. To prepare the grounds for the partnership, local stakeholders and TOI members were interviewed on their individual views of the key sustainability threats in Side. These interviews were then followed by a multi-stakeholder Workshop in April 2002, organised with the support of one of the TOI members, VASCO Travel, and TUDER, the local hotel association. The meeting was attended by the Mayor of Side, representatives of WWF Turkey, and representatives of the private sector, including the Manavgat Chamber of Commerce (MATSO), individual hoteliers, excursion providers and local travel agencies. Several TOI members, along with representatives of UNEP, UNESCO and WTO/ OMT, were also present.

The meeting gave the participants the opportunity to share their views on the main threats to sustainability in the Side region and ways to address these. The participants agreed on three priority actions:

— Waste management (with a focus on waste separation and recycling).

— Education and training on sustainable tourism in hotels, bars and restaurants.

— Promotion of Side's culture and cultural activities.

The participants also agreed on the benefit of a continuous dialogue between tour operators and local stakeholders. During follow up meetings with local stakeholders, a detailed plan of action was developed, and a locally based coordinator was appointed, financed by the Side administration and TUDER. Activities implemented in the two years include:

— A waste separation scheme has been designed and is now in operation in the municipality of Side. Recycling companies have been identified and pick-up times for participating hotels have been set.

— The local recycling company posts signs on its vehicles to promote the Side initiative, and hotels and restaurants post signs at their entrances.

— The Side Tourism Association (TUDER) has placed containers for collecting used batteries in every Side hotel, in the Ali Ihsan Barut elementary school and in the Tourism Hotel Vocational High School.

— Waste separation bins for organic and recyclable waste have been placed in Side for use by residents and tourists.

— Training sessions on solid waste management and waste separation techniques, organised with technical input and background material from UNEP, were held for managers and staff at hotels, apartment hotels and pensions; Side Municipality sanitation workers; sanitation manager and association presidents; members of the Garment Association and of the Bar and Restaurant Association.

Today, over 100 hotels and all local shops and restaurants participate in the waste separation scheme. Data from the last seven months of 2003 are promising: 276 tons of inorganic waste, and 11.978 batteries were collected. Moreover, the new land fill area has been identified and approved and it will be in operations in Summer 2004.

A second TOI partnership has been initiated with Bayahibe, PuntaCana and Bavaro, three of the most visited destinations in the Dominican Republic. Following informal discussions and visits, a Sustainable Tourism Round Table was convened in December 2003, in collaboration with the Bayahibe-La Romana Hotel Association and the Punta Cana Group. The Round Table was also made possible thanks to the financial and technical contribution of the German Technical Cooperation (GTZ), and Conservation International's Center for Environmental Leadership in Business. The participants of the Round Table committed to an Agenda for Action, that include:

— Establishment of a 'Garbage free' zone,

— Improved management of the marine excursions to Isla Saona in Parque del Este,

— Process for greater community involvement,

— Support by tour operators of a promotional programme for the hoteliers in Bayahibe that implement social and environmental programmes.

Participants agreed also on the creation of a Co-ordinating Body that include the Bayahibe-La Romana Hotel Association, the Del Este Hotels Association, the associations of Excursion and local tour operators, the Punta Cana Ecological Foundation, the Bavaro Reef Fund, Ecoparques, the office of the Archbishop of La Altagracia, and the Tour Operators' Initiative. The Co-ordinating Body will oversee the implementation of the agenda and support the continuous communication and co-ordination of actions among all players.

People's Practicipation

Unravelling the identity and structure of different stakeholder groups can be time consuming and the results are not obvious. For example, different agencies can be involved in the management of a site and have different goals and objectives. In many cases, several agencies control various sections of a protected World Heritage site, each with its own management strategy. While sharing a common heritage resource, visitor management strategies and issues vary from one area to the next. Some stakeholders are unwilling to support wider participation, especially when it is seen as a threat to their authority. For example, managers may accept a policy of openness and communication but may resist supplying all pertinent information to interest groups. This situation eventually creates a climate of distrust, limiting the site manager's ability to deal with the public.

The most vocal critics can dominate the participation process. Many citizens view public participation as a means of influencing policies and decisions. Public hearings can become forums in which the most vocal critics of a plan can dominate discussions and exclude others from the process. This can happen if an organised lobby group is heavily represented. Some people with legitimate concerns may be intimidated by a venue such as a meeting hall and be afraid to speak up. Alternative venues such as community centres can facilitate a more comfortable exchange of ideas and encourage balanced communication among stakeholders.

Large numbers of people may be overlooked because they are not as vocal as other groups. Any issue that generates public interest is subject to a wide range of opinion. While most people will have an opinion, many will not feel strongly about the issue. This large majority risks being ignored. It may be felt that they are the group that can be most influenced because they are not very interested and are probably not well informed. The possibility of some event igniting the interest of this less-interested majority should however not be underestimated. Consideration of these groups is essential to ensuring long-term public support.

Hierarchical structures may inhibit stakeholder participation in decision making. In many societies the formal structure of institutions and organisations as well as cultural norms may make it difficult to elicit the opinions of certain groups making stakeholder participation in formal meetings impossible. A few powerful agencies may dominate, overwhelming other stakeholders and blocking cooperation. In some countries, the government is directly involved in the actual business of tourism, functioning as tour operators as well as making policy, which may lead to imbalances in stakeholder input.

Public participation may be more a form of appeasement than a way to solicit stakeholders' input. Offering local communities the opportunity to participate raises expectations about acceptance of their suggestions. A government may try to guide a particular choice either by representing only one opinion or by proposing a set of choices among which only one is tenable. Decisions may have already been made before public participation begins; any changes may be minor with relatively small impacts.

Before embarking on a participatory planning exercise, proponents have to be ready to change original plans according to the input received.

Overemphasis on involving stakeholder groups can lead to a failure to recognise certain effects on resources. Managers must understand how stakeholders perceive impacts and define acceptability. However, many stakeholder groups have limited knowledge about natural and cultural resources and may be unaware of potential negative impacts. Visitors adapt to deteriorating environmental conditions, accepting degradation as the inevitable result of increasing visitation. The visitors who are displeased by the degradation may not return and are not captured by surveys and public involvement efforts.

Other stakeholder groups may be concerned only with economic considerations that could outweigh the desire to protect resources. So, while public participation is necessary, over-reliance on public input can lead to inaction and a deterioration of conditions over time. With resource bases declining and the demand for recreation and tourist attractions on the rise, it is managers who must ultimately decide the parameters of how much and what kinds of tourism activity are acceptable.

Trust is the crucial element of successful public participation. Building trust and a willingness to participate depends on several factors. Positive earlier interaction builds trust. The history of the experiences with, for example, a state government agency influences the chances of fostering participation. Rebuilding relations between conservation authorities and local people after a history of policing and exclusion can be difficult. H.S. Panwar, who taught at the Wildlife Institute of India at Dehra Dun, reported that the main criteria of success in ecologically oriented development projects were building trust and enrolling the full participation of local people in the planning and implementation process.

Honouring commitments builds trust. Amboseli National Park in Kenya, La Amistad National Park in Costa Rica and Panama, and Yellowstone National Park in the United States have all had problems with local communities after funding cuts that forced policy changes. At Amboseli, a lack of funding for maintaining pumps at watering facilities caused a gap in trust with park officials and impinged on the needs of local Maasai cattle herders.

At La Amistad and Yellowstone, personnel and budget cuts took a financial toll on the local communities. Gestures that show equality, for example, sharing information equally among stakeholders, promote trust. From its inception, the Great Barrier Reef project worked from a scientific information base, regularly issuing maps, data and carefully prepared information to the public.

Time is necessary to build trust. Many experts agree that more time and effort could be spent addressing the various agendas of interest groups. One researcher writes, "Trust-building takes time. The history of rural development initiatives is littered with enough examples to indicate that such time is a resource well spent in terms of effective policy outcomes." A non-partisan image helps build trust with stakeholders. When a particular problem arises at a site, the site manager — who is seen as a government official-may be wise to ask a popular local personality to explain the matter to the public.

If time and money permit, credible scientific information can serve as non-partisan evidence to heighten public understanding of an issue and change people's minds. Yellowstone officials published pertinent scientific information, viewed as more neutral, in the daily newspaper to advise the public about a project to reintroduce wolves into the park.

A process calling for participation and collaboration has been found to be more conducive to consensus than traditional methods involving expert planners only. Work in community extension projects has shown more progress in community relations when participatory methods are used. Experts report that no point is too early in the project cycle to begin inviting local participation. A participatory approach is beneficial in several ways:

— While issues of power and control will not disappear certain individuals will always be motivated to convert others to their position the participatory process enhances communication by showing both the common ground and the differences between the stakeholder groups. The exercise often leads to compromise and a breakdown of defensive positions.
— Evidence suggests that people are reluctant to divulge past difficulties. Informal communication systems such as surveys can help get people to reveal their interests and concerns. Reports from the North Pennines Tourism Partnership programme in England revealed that such informal communication helped to resolve issues between the different groups.
— Public involvement tends to build momentum towards collaborative implementation. As one researcher has pointed out, misunderstandings between groups, rather than a lack of information, is at the core of many social difficulties.

Communication Techniques

Participatory techniques such as rural appraisals allow local people to describe their environment. Participatory Rural Appraisals (PRAs) can facilitate the exchange of informal information between local government officials, NGO staff and local people. These methods have proven capable of overcoming the problems of listening and shaping an accurate assessment of stakeholder concerns. The techniques help map out local resources, ways people make a living, trends in resource use, and the local costs and benefits of conservation and protection. They are practical methods of encouraging local participation, fostering communication and making a more accurate appraisal of local concerns. The utility of these methods has been demonstrated in many areas of the world, particularly in Pakistan and India. Participatory techniques, including PRAs, can be used for both natural and cultural sites.

Alternative forms of dialogue can help limit public confrontations. Public meetings can be ineffective when the parties with the most vested interests attend with the goal of pressing their particular causes. Less confrontational meeting structures can reduce such undue influence and limit the posturing of interest groups for the press. During the controversial Yellowstone wolf reintroduction project, open houses were held where individual people could sit down in a relaxed atmosphere and talk directly with representatives of the various agencies involved. Special meetings were held to allow powerful interest groups to voice their opinions, but they were listening sessions only. These were run by female park officials, perceived as less threatening and non-partisan than male officials, and local police were hired to maintain order.

The process of developing a management plan can encourage the participation of stakeholders. The process can also be used to build consensus. However, instead of releasing draft management plans for public comment, planners should begin by identifying what is needed from the public, and what a site can offer them in return. Plans and strategies should be developed slowly, be dynamic and adaptable, and be concise rather than lengthy. Above all, they should be inclusive of all stakeholders. Examples of successful issue-based management planning include the great Smokey Mountains National Park in the United

States, where many trails were in poor condition and needed to be closed to have time to recover. Park managers realised that closing trails would generate negative sentiment.

To educate the public about the situation, management decided to involve people in the process. Meetings were held to give people an understanding of the park's mission and to provide them with an opportunity to participate in setting priorities. At the Willandra Lakes Region World Heritage site, in Australia, a five-day workshop was held at which community members helped write the first draft of a management plan. The exercise guaranteed continued support for the plan. At the Shark Bay World Heritage site, also in Australia, participatory management plans for conservation areas are also made available for public comment for at least two months, a practice required under Western Australian law.

An advisory group or stakeholders' organisation can play a crucial role in the success of management objectives. Consultation with various interest groups through regular meetings and public workshops offers opportunities for stakeholders to comment on a preliminary management plan. This relationship enables site managers to bring local people into decision-making. Ongoing conflicts will not necessarily go away, but an advisory group provides a structure for the problem-solving process so that conflicts and solutions can be identified more clearly. Public participation is more likely to be effective and sustained through stakeholder groups than through individual participation.

4

Hospitality Business Promotion

In some communities, shopping has become so important that it is the number one tourism attraction and in those "shopping centric" communities people come specifically for the purpose of shopping. This urge to shop is not new. In fact, shopping was an important activity as far back as Biblical days and played an essential role in the development of medieval community life. The month of December is the premier shopping month in a good part of the world. After meals and lodging they spending most money on:

— T-shirts, sweatshirts, and other clothes with a name or design representing the location or attraction

— Crafts

— Local food products (not meals)

Almost 70% buy gifts ahead of time for holidays, birthdays, and similar events.

Shopping, however, is more than merely exchanging money for goods; it also provides a window into the soul of a community. Many visitors in fact use shopping as one of the ways by which they judge your community or attraction. The decision to return to a community is often based less on the quality of its lodging or events than it is on the shopping experience had while the person was in the community. Shopping also acts as a marketing tool for a community or attraction. When someone says that he/she bought an item in a particular place, that person is subtly, yet often effectively, advertising not only the item but also the place of purchase.

Following are some important points to promote your community's or attraction's shopping experience:

— Tourism shopping is most successful when you offer items that are unique. Too many tourism centers have become so standardised that visitors may wonder why they ever left home. Develop a listing of places that sell local or unique products. Connect the sale of these products to your local theme or motto. Encourage shop owners to stress this theme not only with the products that they sell but also with the appearance of their store or locale.

— If you cannot compete in price, compete in quality and service. Often merchants complain that they cannot compete against the buying power of the large chain and retail/wholesale discount stores. The basic rule of thumb is: "Do not fight a war that you cannot win." In other words, rather than compete on price, local stores should compete on customer service, a willingness to find local products and promote these products while offering outstanding service. For example, the telephone should never take priority over a customer. Make sure that every customer is greeted with a smile and even if the customer buys nothing, develop a relationship so that he/she or a friend may return.

— Keep regular and convenient business hours. Often store owners, especially in smaller communities forget that they are there to serve the public and not vice versa. Hours should be kept according to the posted sign. Most importantly, highly successful businesses are those that are open when people want to shop.

For example, in the United States the two busiest shopping days are Saturdays and Sundays. These days are followed by, the "shoulder days" of Mondays and Fridays in importance. Yet in too many communities stores are closed on Sundays and Mondays while being open on the off days of Tuesday, Wednesday and Thursday.

— Remind your city workers and law enforcement that they are an important part of the shopping experience. Communities can only survive if they make money. It is important for city/community workers to encourage people to go downtown to shop, develop ways so that people are not fined for parking, and know what stores and products are available in their community. Every city employee should see him/herself as a community ambassador. The more that public officials support and promote local shopping, the healthier the local economy will tend to be.

— People shop where merchants know their niche markets. Often communities have no idea who is shopping in their community. Good service also means meeting the needs of your customers. For example, if your costumers come from specific age or linguistic groups, try to provide service in their language or give them the type of attention that will make people want to buy. Tourism people can be of tremendous aid to local merchants by sharing visitor profiles with them.

— Too many tourism and travel products are rich in hype and low on product delivery. The worst thing in the world is to get someone to visit your locale and discover that you cannot deliver what you promised. The best advertising in the world will not compensate for a poor product. If you are a community, do a full outside assessment and then advertise only what you have. If you are an attraction, review what you offer each year. Is the admission price and time investment worth the visit?

— Find alternative ways to market your products so that people will shop at your local stores. Instead of spending a great deal of money on good advertising, consider spending more money on personnel development and creating a better level of customer service. Most tourism officials already know that the best advertising is word-of-mouth advertising. Create a paradigm shift that sees advertising as one part of a total marketing strategy. While being the best product may not insure success, good person to person skills combined with good products are helpful in gaining success.

— Train! Train! and then, train some more! All too often shopkeepers believe that they are offering good customer service, only to find out that their employees are not translating the owner's vision into actions. The higher the quality of training, the better your product. Bring in experts to train people all over your community. Seek ways to get the entire community on-board by training everyone from security personnel to front line people. Ask these people about the training that they would like to have and then provide it.

The tourists look for crafts to use and display in their home. They also enjoy seasonal and holiday items. Their favorite craft medium is wood, followed by nature materials and fabric. Over 50% of the tourists used these sources to find crafts in a community or within the state: tourist brochures or state travel packets; local shops; magazines or newspaper articles; travel magazines and guide books; people who have been there before; directory or map of art or craft locations or events; information at the hotel, either written or from hotel personnel; local residents; and ads in local papers. They made less use of travel agents, tour guides, or telephone books for this information.

Tourists are most likely to shop for crafts at craft fairs and festivals, craft shops, and gift shops carrying both crafts and other types of gift products. Many enjoy shopping in a historic house typical of the region or shop with a rustic appearance.

While tourists find a large selection of crafts filling every nook and cranny of a shop is desirable, they appreciate neatly arranged displays to bring a sense of order. Displays featuring ways to use and display crafts in the home help sell crafts since some tourists want assistance visualising ways to use crafts in their homes. Tourists want written information on care, safety, materials used, and ways to use the craft items. Tourists value sales personnel who let them browse, who initiate pleasant conversation, and who can provide information about the craft producer and craft technique.

Tourists expect to shop when they travel. This chart shows: 1) the products they generally buy, and 2) categories on which they spend the most money. Retailers appealing to tourists might use this information to plan merchandise assortments, promotional activities, and pricing strategies. Communities might also use this information to help evaluate the mix of businesses serving tourist needs in their towns.

Tourism Styles

By choice or by necessity, many communities, especially rural ones, have focused their tourist attractions and other supporting businesses and services on a limited range of activities. Knowing as much as possible about the interests of travelers to specialised tourist areas can help you invest your time and money in efforts that appeal to your visitors and result in increased profit for your business and community.

So, in addition to studying the tourists in a general way, there are four specialised tourism styles among the tourists. People in each tourism style enjoyed similar travel activities and shopping opportunities. They reacted in similar ways to words describing craft themes and types of craft producers. They used similar criteria when they bought crafts. A tourist might adopt more than one of these tourism styles depending on where she or he is traveling and what's available.

Ethnic, Arts, and People Style

Ethnic, Arts, and People tourists are actively involved in their tourism. They immerse themselves in the community. For them, tourism is an opportunity for education and personal development. It's a time for experiencing authenticity in a community and its way of life. They actively:

— Visit ethnic communities

— Participate in community festivals

— Visit art galleries and museums

— Attend concerts and the theater

— Interact with local residents

Products they buy:

— Crafts

— Local food products (does not include meals)

— Antiques Books about the area they are visiting

They are attracted to timeless crafts such as:

— Ethnic crafts

— Folk art

— Designer crafts

— Traditional crafts of the region

Specifically they look for:

— Crafts that can be used in the home

— Jewelry

— Crafts to add to their collections

Criteria for selecting crafts:

— Appealing color, design, and quality workmanship

— Items that are unique and represent new ideas

— Crafts made by well-known artisans who sign their work

Sources for finding crafts:

— Printed materials such as directories or maps of craftperson's studios

— Brochures at museums

— Suggestions from local residents and shops

Places they shop for crafts:

— Art gallery or museum shops

— Antique shops

— Booths at craft fairs, festivals, bazaars, and flea markets

— Craftperson's studio or workshop

Preferred craft shopping environment:

— Shops with rustic appearance

— Historic houses

— Artisans demonstrating their work

History and Parks Style

The History and Parks tourists are introspective. They devote time to enjoying scenery, contemplating a sense of place, reflecting on the past, and photographing the experience. They take time to plan their trips. They visit:

— Historic sites and homes
— Museums
— Recreated villages that depict a past way of life
— Gardens
— State and national parks

Products they buy:

— Crafts
— Postcards
— Books about the area and its history
— Local food products
— Items to add to their collections

They like crafts with these themes:

— Regional
— Historic
— Ethnic
— Nature
— Country
— Western

They look especially for crafts they can display in their homes. Criteria for selecting crafts are:

— Appealing color, design, and quality workmanship
— Clever ideas
— Can display in the home
— Easy care
— Easy to pack
— Includes the name or theme related to site

Sources for finding crafts:

- Travel packets from state tourism bureaus prior to a trip
- Materials available at tourist sites

Places they shop for crafts:

- Parks and tourist sites
- Theme parks
- Tourist visitor centers
- Highway or rest stops
- Craft shops and gift shops
- Craft fairs, festivals, bazaars, and flea markets
- Craftperson's studio or workshop
- Art gallery or museum shop

Active Outdoor Style

Active Outdoor tourists are outdoor enthusiasts who vigorously enjoy parks and nature areas. They actively:

- Hike and backpack
- Camp
- Fish
- Sail and boat
- Hunt
- Swim
- Ski
- Play tennis or golf

Products they buy:

- T-shirts and sweatshirts with a name or design related to the location

Crafts are not a major focus. When they do select crafts they prefer products made from nature materials such as grasses, corn husks, pine cones, dried flowers, and stone. These themes are appealing:

— Rural

— Western

— Recreation

— Folk art

— Traditional themes

Criteria for selecting crafts:

— Can display in their homes

— Humor

— Name or design related to the location

— Made by well-known craftperson

— Is signed, marked, or a limited edition

Places they shop for crafts:

— General store serving a resort or camping area

— Gas station or convenience store

— Parks or recreation gift shop

Urban Entertainment Style

Urban Entertainment tourists visit cities where they are constantly on the go, day and night. Social interaction is important to these travellers. Many use packaged tours. These are young men and women with higher incomes. They travel extensively in the U.S. They enthusiastically:

— "Shop til they drop."

— Attend professional sports events

— Visit recreational theme parks

— Go dancing and nightclubbing

They look for products with the name or design representing their vacation location. They buy:

— T-shirts and sweatshirts

— Souvenir items such as pens, bumper stickers, and key chains

— Crafts

They prefer general craft themes such as:

— Handicrafts

— Designer crafts

— Contemporary crafts

— Western themes

They look specifically for crafts with visual impact:

— Crafts to display in their homes

— Seasonal or holiday decorations

— Clothes, accessories, or jewelry to wear

Criteria for selecting crafts:

— Ease of care and cleaning

— Items that are new, innovative, limited edition, signed

— Humor

— Name or design related to the location or attraction

Sources for finding crafts:

— Hotel staff

— Printed materials in hotel rooms or at hotel desks

Places they shop for crafts:

— They shop everywhere:

— Hotels and restaurants

— Theme parks

— Sports centers
— Visitor centers
— Gas stations
— Clothing and accessory boutiques
— Craftperson's studio or workshop

They are attracted to shops with either crowded or modern appearances. Successful craft producers promoted themselves and their products by:

— providing business cards and hang tags
— signing their work
— using a logo
— offering limited edition information
— providing written biographical data

Successful craft producers used more wholesale channels, including:

— direct sale to retailers
— trade/wholesale shows
— selling to retailers at craft fairs
— sales representatives
— mail order ads to retailers

Higher income producers:

— Worked an average of 55 hours per week, considerably more than those in lower income groups;
— Concentrated on a particular medium or technique, offering fewer types of items in their product line;
— Identified themselves as: artist, artist/craftsman, and designer/craftsman. Producers in the lower income group called themselves artisan, craftsman, folk artist, and handicrafter;

— Were 66.7% male. Men contributed a higher percentage to household income. On average, their most expensive items were 4 times the price of those of women; their least expensive items were twice the price of those of women.

If you wish to increase your income:

— Review your promotional practices;
— Target communities, attractions, shops, and craft fairs serving the tourism styles most compatible with your products;
— Target the wholesale market place to get your products to tourist communities;
— Review your price structure;
— Review the type of product you produce in relation to tourist demand;
— Continue to develop your capacity to be original, create your own designs;
— Stay abreast of the number of people producing crafts similar to yours;
— Review your professional practices and work habits;
— Stay alert to tourist interests.

Strategies for Marketing Crafts

Identifying a target market may be difficult for retailers wanting to cater to both local residents and tourists. Retailers cannot necessarily apply knowledge of their local customers' purchasing habits to tourists. Knowing what retailers in tourist areas are doing to market crafts can help you review your business plan with the tourist market in mind.

Retailers viewed tourism as important to the local area and to the state's economy. Attracting more tourists was seen as a good idea. However, retailers did not necessarily view their state as a tourist state or interesting for tourists. Nor did they have an understanding of their role with tourists. Feelings about the attractiveness or pull of their state are communicated by retailers in direct contact with tourists. Retailers knowledgeable about the resources, history, and products of their area are better able to serve tourists and market products to tourists.

When selecting their craft inventory, retailers considered criteria that were similar to those used by tourists. Those were appealing design and color, quality of workmanship, price, and newness or innovation. Retailers are encouraged to explore whether tourists associate a particular craft with a local historic site, ethnic festival, or attraction. Most retailers perceived that tourists traveling through their state did not associate a particular type of craft with the state; however, tourists tend to view **crafts and other objects purchased during travel as having symbolic value**. These products may be among tourists' most valued possessions as reminders of their travel experiences.

Retailers were most likely to use visual displays of the crafts and direct customer contact as selling techniques. Advertising was done primarily through print media. Over half of the retailers held special events to promote craft sales, such as open houses, special shows, seasonal events, and in-house classes or demonstrations. Retailers did not seem to rely on brochures for advertising, although tourists preferred brochures for information on crafts.

Careful analysis of activities of tourists in the area and the enroute tourists may reflect a seasonal pattern or suggest days and hours when tourists want to shop. Although most retailers reported that they were open all year for business, their busiest months were June through August and November and December. January through March were the slowest months for selling crafts. Tourist departments, travel centers, lodging and resort facilities, and Chambers of Commerce might provide additional insight on general tourist patterns.

Retailers need to think about the possibility of tourists as a targeted consumer group. Target marketing, used in conjunction with the four tourism styles, has potential for retailers who would like to increase their sales to tourists. Many tourists value "uniqueness" in the crafts they select and retailers tended to focus on the uniqueness or novelty of their products. However, uniqueness alone may not be enough if the product isn't right for the target market.

A strong working relationship between the craft producer and the retailer can result in increased profits for both parties. The relationship can be strengthened by a better understanding of how they make initial contacts with one another, what incentives they offer, how they work together on pricing, and what problems they encounter in the relationship.

Craft producers typically contact retailers directly. They learn about retailers through other craft producers and by contacts at fairs and shows.

Craft retailers offered these incentives to producers:

— special care of the product and safe-guards to prevent theft and damage

— quick payment

— knowledgeable sales help

Craft producers looked for retailers who offered quick payment, location in a tourist area, adequate space to display their work, and a favorable percentage of the consignment price. Craft producers provided these incentives to retailers:

— volume discounts

— deferred payments

— exclusivity of product line

— easy exchange of items

Retailers wanted more information about the craft producer and the product. Most retailers purchased crafts on a wholesale and/or consignment basis.

— Retailers carried craft items an average of six months.

— Over half the retailers returned 70 to 80 percent of the retail price to consignor.

— Most retailers worked in conjunction with the craftperson to set the retail price for consignment.

— Most retailers determined on the wholesale price of crafts according to the craft based on past selling history.

Retailers identified problems with craft producers related to:

— overpriced products

— unsteady source of supply from season to season

Craft producers identified problem with retailers such as:

— retailers slow to pay

— taking too large a percentage on consignment

— keeping poor records

— going out of business

— lost or stolen items

Recommendations to Craft Producers

— Create incentives for retailers with volume discount, deferred payments, exclusivity of product line, and easy exchange of items.

— Evaluate your ability to produce products in relationship to the amount of orders accepted.

— Explain your wholesale price to retailers, in terms related to design, quality, innovativeness, and timeliness.

— Provide retailers with information about yourself and your product. Sign your work. Consider producing limited editions.

— Discuss with the retailer your availability for demonstrations, receptions, and special showings.

— Work with craft retailers as to the best way to display and/or demonstrate your products.

Recommendations to Retailers

— Develop a consistent pay schedule and keep producers informed of any changes.

— Explain carefully your process for consigning and pricing items.

— Evaluate your methods of bookkeeping for efficiency and accuracy related to inventory control and payment.

— Review and improve precautions to prevent loss, theft, and damage to items.

Tourists enjoy travel as a total experience; therefore, community-wide cooperation is necessary to take advantage of the strong link between what tourists like to do and what they like to buy. Consider your business and your goals for taping the tourist market as you decide which of these suggestions offer the greatest potential benefit for you.

Understand your Tourists

How can you learn about tourists and use that information to your advantage—and theirs? Consider these ideas as a community or as an individual business operator.

— Listen to tourists talk about your community to understand why they find it so interesting.
— Review the four tourism styles and determine which types are most likely to visit your community.
— Evaluate the services and products in your community to see if they correspond with interests of the tourists most likely to visit.
— Identify new businesses or services to expand the experience of tourists. For example, if your community has an ethnic heritage or annual festival, could you organise ways for visitors to interact with local residents via home visits for coffee or dinner?
— If your community does not have gift or craft shops, consider ways to satisfy tourists' desires to shop such as selling crafts and other products in general stores, gas stations, and convenience stores.

Consider whether your merchandise "fits" the types of tourists your community attracts. Examples:

1. Books on traditional crafts and craft producers for—Historic and Parks and Ethnic, Arts, and People tourists;
2. Film or blank videotape for Historic and Parks tourists.

Evaluate your craft product line, your promotion methods, and pricing strategies. Consider:

1. Producing or carrying items for which perceived tourist demand exceeds availability;
2. Including popular gift price ranges - $5-10, $10-20, and $20-30;
3. Localising products by incorporating a name or design motif that is related to the attraction or location.

Customer Services

A customer service orientation is one of the most important strategies you can employ among businesses, tourist attractions, and residents to enhance tourists' experiences in your community. Increase the customer service orientation of your sales personnel.

- Encourage them to engage customers in friendly conversation, at the same time being alert to when customers want to browse alone;
- Provide training so sales personnel can explain craft techniques, talk about craft producers, and suggest ways to use and display crafts at home;
- Alert them to items that make good gifts and to the attributes (both aesthetic and practical) that make the items appealing.
- Consider value added services which make the purchasing process easier for tourists. These include services like gift wrap, shipping, monogramming, and acceptance of credit cards.
- Provide written information for tourists on care, safety, and use of crafts; materials used to produce the craft, particularly those of local origin; history or tradition of the craft; and information on the craft producer.
- Let tourists know if crafts are signed, marked, or in limited edition.
- Display crafts to show a variety of ways to use and display them at home. For example, display clay pitchers to illustrate multiple uses: to serve lemonade, to hold flowers, and to add to a grouping of decorative items.
- Periodically change in-store visual displays and promotional materials to reflect new trends.

How can your community work together to help visitors enjoy spending time—and money—in your community? Being involved in your community's tourism organisation is one way you can help this happen.

— Seek representation from all aspects of your community.

— Don't overlook retailers, craft producers, gas station operators, residents, and others who come in contact with tourists.

— Identify the local attractions, products, and crafts that make your community or area unique.

— Plan advertising and promotional efforts around the target tourism styles.

— Appeal to tourists through signs and promotional materials by using terms tourists use to describe desirable themes: Western, designer, etc. Note differences among tourism styles.

— Become well-known in your community so community businesses and residents can promote your business.

— Plan strategies to promote attractions, crafts, and other local products and services in a cooperative way.

— Develop a list of local craft producers and producers of specialised local products.

— Develop an active referral system among the community's businesses and attractions to market what your community has to offer to tourists. Exchange supplies of brochures, business cards, etc. to distribute to visitors.

— Develop cooperative displays among businesses, at tourist attractions, or in public display areas combining items that your target tourists often buy. For example, for Ethnic, Arts, and People tourists combine crafts, local foods, antiques, and books about the area.

— Publicise communities, crafts, and other specialty products in places tourists look for information, e.g. tourist brochures, state tourism packets, magazine and newspaper articles, travel magazines and guidebooks, hotels and restaurants.

— Review advertising opportunities in local newspapers and in tourist brochures, magazines, and guidebooks.

Hospitality Training

Hospitality training can build awareness about an area's specialty products and crafts as well as inform participants about attractions and teach skills for assisting visitors. Potential participants include anyone in the community who has contact with tourists-employees and managers/owners of restaurants, hotels, B&Bs, shops, gas stations, tourist attractions, other local businesses, and local residents. To help mold hospitality training to the needs of your community, assess retailers, craft producers, hospitality services, other businesses, community organisations, and residents on their:

1. Attitudes toward their community as an interesting place to visit;
2. Knowledge about local attractions, resources, craft producers, local products, and services of interest to tourists.

In your hospitality training include information about the community's ethnic background and traditions, crafts and craft producers, local foods, antiques.

Agritourism

An increasing number of farm businesses are opening their

doors to visitors today. Farm tours, farm-based Bed and Breakfast operations, farm vacations, seasonal festivals, and other forms of agritourism are attracting growing numbers of local, regional and even international visitors. An agritourism enterprise can be a profitable and enjoyable undertaking for some farmers, diversifying the business and creating employment for family members and others.

Agritourism also represents a real opportunity for economic development in some communities. The agritourism industry is relatively undeveloped in New York State compared to some other states, and especially compared to other countries where agritourism is extremely popular among vacationers. There are many opportunities for strengthening agritourism in New York, locally, on the regional level, and statewide.

Enhancing cooperation among agritourism businesses, connecting agritourism with other forms of tourism, creating cooperative promotional programs, building an international presence for NY agritourism, and providing business development assistance and support for new agritourism enterprises are among the strategies that could be pursued.

Some components of the A/T industry are:

1) *Agricultural Products*-Included are fresh fruits and vegetables; trees, shrubs and bedding plants; fresh or smoked fish; and certain processed food (wine, honey, maple syrup, apple cider, cheese, preserves, fruit juices). Agricultural products also include experiences or activities associated with farming (tours by bus, wagon, buggy, sleigh, or foot; vacation farms; rural bed and breakfasts; fishing and hunting; firewood cutting).
2) Tourist-Generally, someone travelling for pleasure and who either stays away from home overnight or is on

a day trip at least an hour's drive one-way from his/her origin; not necessarily someone from out-of-state.

3) Traveller—Similar to "tourist" except that travel can be for any purpose (business, visiting family and friends, conventions, etc.) except commuting to and from work.

4) Non-local-The same as "traveller" and used here to mean anyone whose permanent residence is located one hour or more one-way from the A/T operation; used to distinguish local customers from all others.

5) Agricultural Festivals or Events-Activities that are related to a particular agricultural product as defined above. The Tulip Festival, The National Cherry Festival, and the Asparagus Festival are examples.

Objectives for Attracting Customers

How can you attract non-local customers? Objectives for solving this problem are::

1) Find out how many and what type of agricultural businesses and events attract non-local customers;

2) Learn something about the non-local customers themselves;

3) Determine the total number of non-local customers who buy from direct farm product outlets and how much they spend; and

4) Discover the types of agricultural products travellers are interested in buying and why they do not buy more.

What does the inventory reveal about the state's A/T industry?

First, many of the direct market outlets are already located where they can capture a large portion of the traveller market. However, it appears that only a handful of businesses are doing so. One projects revealed that 17% of the roadside markets and U-Pick businesses surveyed had 93% of the non-local customers in 1983. Eight businesses alone accounted for 57% of the non-local customers! Sixty percent of the businesses sampled had less than 300 non-local customers in 1983; a few had around 100,000 non-locals. Thus, there is room for expansion of all direct outlet types catering to non- local needs, particularly in those areas already receiving a great deal of non-local traffic.

The second finding of the inventory is that having a successful A/T business requires a unique product. There are already a large number of traditional direct farm product outlets in Michigan. What sets yours apart from the rest? To answer this question requires you to adopt a marketing approach for your business, match your business identity (who you are or want to be) with the travelling public's image of you, and position a unique product in travellers' minds. Your aim is to uniquely position your product (produce + special service + atmosphere) in the heads of your target markets.

For example, think about roadside markets. In the customer's mind, most roadside markets seem alike, but there are one or two that stand out from the crowd because of their uniqueness. Your goal should be to be one of those that stands out. However, you cannot be all things to all people. Therefore, select the market or target group you would like to attract and determine what you can offer them that will make them see you as a unique business. This way customers can match themselves with you and know that you will best satisfy their needs.

Here are some things that add to a traveller's experience with farm products: picnic facilities, pleasant surroundings, walking trails, opportunities for children, wagon rides, programmes, tours, educational signs/ exhibits, skiing, lunch, desserts, recipes, newsletters, special events/contests/festivals, announcements, gift certificates, mailing lists, good parking, calendar of events, T-shirts, friendly employees, clear directions, rent-a-tree/plant/shrub, clean restrooms facilities.

Some of these things (for example, wagon rides) raise the question: "How much liability do I incur by providing them." Direct marketers have provided the facilities and services listed above. This list is by no means complete. You can probably think of other things you might do or already are doing. The bottom line is that you need to develop a unique product that is more than just produce. To develop this product, you must look to who you are and who you want to be (your identity).

What's the economic impact of the A/T industry in Michigan? Additional findings from the survey of roadside market and U-Pick businesses indicate:

— There were 2.4 million non-local customers in 1983 (31% of all customers at roadside markets and U-Picks).

— There were $18 million in direct sales to non-locals in 1983. This figure represents 55% of all direct farm product sales in Michigan. It also means that some businesses are selling a large amount of farm products to non-locals (17% of the businesses got 93% of the non- local share in 1983).

— There would be 2,000 fewer part-time and full-time jobs in Michigan if there were no non-local sales at roadside markets and U-Picks.

— 99% of the income received from non-locals is re-spent by roadside market and U-Pick operators in Michigan on everything from fertilisers to containers.

How can these informal sources be used most effectively?

1) Actively hand out attractive, current brochures and other printed material with clear directions and accurate descriptions of your products.

2) Provide a quality product. This includes friendly and knowledgeable employees, a clean site, fresh produce etc..

3) Remember, nearly two-thirds of the non-local customers interviewed were repeat visitors! These people convey information (good or bad) about your business to others.

4) Be sure others in your community are aware of your business. These people can promote for you because travelers ask them to recommend things to do. Work on establishing good relationships with travel information center personnel, lodging and state park employees, gas station attendants, and restaurant workers.

The second way to increase your non-local sales is through cooperation. As an individual, you may not be able to do all that is necessary to reach the traveling public. Therefore, cooperative promotional efforts (mutual signing, radio ads, and so on) among several direct outlets in an area may help stretch tight budgets and reach more customers. Cooperation may also occur between the farming community and organisations on the one hand and tourism agencies, convention bureaus, and chambers of commerce on the other.

The goal of cooperative promotion is to exchange travelers. For example, convention bureaus or chambers of commerce can assist in getting the word out that there are agricultural products and events nearby. Farm employees, in turn, can refer travelers to restaurants, lodging facilities, and other attractions in the area. This means that all employees that come in contact with visitors be well-informed about community resources. Farm trail maps, placemats with a map showing the location of direct outlets, and directories are examples of printed promotional material that has been cooperatively produced in Michigan. A California wine directory, sold at cost, provides travelers with maps and descriptions of wineries, restaurants, and lodging facilities.

Third, be aware of and incorporate into your product the unique characteristics and needs of non-local travelers. There are various subsegments of the non-local market and you must decide which of these you want to attract. Each subsegment has different desires. For example, a business catering primarily to organised bus tours would have some different facilities and promotional methods than one catering primarily to day users from a major metropolitan area. Many direct outlets have a high proportion of repeat business and this makes it possible to establish a loyal market among non-locals.

Generally, travelers are an educated, older, sophisticated group of consumers with money to spend. These people are looking for things to do that tell them something about the area they are visiting—for example, human interest stories, local history, and authentic, locally grown or produced goods. This implies that they will not come back if what they are looking for is not there, and they will let many others know of their disappointment through the powerful word-of-mouth system. These folks are also looking for a recreational experience and something fun to do. Consider such experiences as part of the product you are trying to sell.

Fourth, to attract such customers in large numbers, you must realise that you are in the guest business. This means that direct outlets desiring more non-local business need to have their product ready when guests arrive. That product is no longer the produce. It is the produce plus an experience something that people remember that will make them want to return and tell others about you. In other words, you are no longer just in production. Instead, you need to adopt a marketing approach.

Advertising and Promotion

Information advertising is often used where demand does not presently exist. Advertising can enhance an organisation's image in the long can also remind consumers to keep buying on a regular basis. Coca-Cola is an example of a product at this mature stage. Five decisions must be made in selecting an advertising strategy:

— Set advertising objectives.

— Determine the advertising budget.

— Create the advertising message.

— Select the advertising media.

— Evaluate the advertising results.

Cost is likely to be most serious constraint. However, it is important to understand the range of approaches that exist. This is particularly true given the pressures to move beyond standard forms of advertising in order to gain attention in crowded marketplace. Understanding options available to the competition can also enhance your own campaign.

Advertising Objectives

Advertising objectives flow from previous marketing decisions about your product, target market, image, and knowledge of the competition. Decide whether the message is persuasive, informational, image building, or a reminder. Outline exactly what you want the advertising programme to accomplish. Mention a specific target market and a time frame to achieve it. The new owner of a gift shop may objective to "bring in 300 new customers from the nearby resorts within two months to introduce them new retail offerings." A rural community might target Fargo-Moorhead residents with the objective of increasing attendance at a September harvesting festival.

Advertising Budget

Options for determining an advertising budget fall into four basic categories: investment, affordable, competitive, percent of sales. The best (and least used) way to set an advertising budget is to view advertising dollars as an investment. Advertising must increase profit margins to more than offset advertising expenditures. Costs must be tied to results to avoid draining profits and reserves. Set objectives, then define the tasks required to accomplish this goal, and determine the cost of performing those tasks.

The universal advice in all business sectors is to consider advertising as a necessary expenditure, like interest payments and utilities, to assure the health of the business. It is not a luxury to be cut first when revenues decline. What you would like to invest and what you can afford rarely match. A budget based on "what I can afford" is certainly a critical question for most in the tourism sector. However, using funds "leftover" after paying other bills makes for a very unstable and uncertain operating environment. Long-range planning is difficult.

A low priority on advertising also ignores the effect of marketing on sales volume. The compromise is to work through a budget analysis by another method, and then to adjust advertising objectives if costs exceed available funds. Private firms and communities differ so widely that it quickly becomes meaningless to compare advertising budgets. Comparison is defensive rather than aggressive.

Percent of sales is often touted as a simple way to calculate advertising budgets. A fixed dollar amount is set annually based on previous sales, and then allocated to individual advertising components; for example, newspaper ads and brochures. However, there are no hard and fast rules for selecting a percentage, and this strategy ignores unexpected opportunities that could arise such as a late snowfall or a "hot" trend. Instead money is distributed on the basis of availability. A serious drawback of the percentage method is if revenues fall, you will spend less at a time when you need to devote more resources to advertising.

Investigate other resources to supplement available funds. The Minnesota Office of Tourism administers a joint venture marketing programme. Advertising campaigns may be eligible for matching funds allocated on a competitive basis to any local, regional, or statewide nonprofit tourism organisation formed to promote tourism. You might also be able to work out trade arrangements with the media where you exchange advertising time or space for the travel services you offer.

Advertising Message

Marketing a service, like travel opportunities, is very different from selling a tangible product like a car. One fundamental difference is that tourism depends largely on the personalities of the people who deliver the travel experience—the people who meet and greet guests. It can not be controlled the way circumstances surrounding the purchase of weekly grocery items can be controlled. There are also different rewards for the consumer. Usually people vacation experiences because of emotional rewards rather than purely rational reasons.

An advertising message from a creative endeavour that tries to reach a customer whose travel expectations may be complex. Travel's personal nature and emotional appeal shape the advertising message. It is important to make key points prominent in your advertising message. Many things could be said about any product, and probably an unlimited variety for travel destinations. No ad should attempt to say it all: say a few well. To set your business or community apart, there might be times when it is appropriate to concentrate on only one feature. Talk to your guests, to the experts, and even to competitors to determine what is distinctive about your operations or offerings.

Some suggestions on creating the advertising message are:

— Spotlight unique differences you offer.
— Facts are better than generalities. "As low as $399" is better than saying "reasonably priced."
— Don't shy away from ads with lots of text if what you have to say is important in selling your product. Image advertising is an exception to this.
— Alleviate anxiety about going to a new place. In Minnesota, travellers may be lukewarm about going to a new destination, or to the North Woods where lodging and eating are unknown.
— Use research to test daring new ideas, and don't be afraid to try. Don't follow and mimic: create and lead.
— Stress quality, quality, quality in ad appearance and content.

Generally, the size, extent, and nature of tourism impacts depend upon:

— volume of tourist activity relative to local activity
— length and nature of tourist contacts with the community
— degree of concentration/dispersal of tourist activity in the area
— similarities or differences between local populations and tourists
— stability/sensitivity of local economy, environment, and social structure
— how well tourism is planned, controlled, and managed.

— Look at both the benefits and costs of any proposed actions. While tourism development can increase income, revenues, and employment, it also involves costs. Evaluate benefits and costs of tourism development from the perspectives of local government, businesses, and residents.

— Bargains are still irresistible.

— If there's news -"the first," "the only"- treat it as news and feature it prominently in the ad. The Minnesota Explorer newspaper of the Minnesota Office of Tourism uses this strategy.

— Use coupons as more than just clip- outs in one corner of the ad. Make the coupon the focus of your ad, or write more information on the coupon. Often, the coupon is the only thing that gets read.

— Photographs gain a lot of attention and should be captioned.

Advertisements are evaluated with the AIDA principle attention, interest, desire, and action. First be sure that potential guests look at an ad, and then that they are interested enough to read on. A good ad will create a desire or need for the product and motivate action.

Media Selection

Media selection means finding the most cost-effective way to deliver the message to the desired audience. Reach, frequency, and impact are key concepts in selecting the combination of media used. Each is the number of people exposed to your message. Frequency is the number of times they are exposed to the message. Impact is the quality of the exposure in terms of consumer response. Remember that advertising deals with cumulative effects.

Visitor response usually comes from a variety of media used long time span.

A wide variety of options exist for timing your media campaign. You can send out your advertising message continuously, in concentrated small "bursts," or at regular intervals. Remember that vacation decisions are usually made well in advance of actual travel. Coupled with media production schedules set well in advance, a very long planning horizon becomes necessary for media buys. Know your target audience's media habits.

Consider the type message you want to convey. For example, an upcoming special event needs the immediacy of television and radio coverage. Yet, a detailed tour package is best presented in written format. Advertising costs are a major consideration. Cost per thousand (CPM) is a useful concept in judging alternative media strategies. Cost per thousand is defined as the cost to deliver one full page black and white ad to 1,000 households.

Newspaper Advertising

Newspapers contain both classified and display advertising. Classifieds charge by the inch, word, or line. Most of the tourism industry finds display ads, billed on the basis of the column inch, more effective. A column inch spans a single column about 2 inches wide and 1 inch deep. Advertisers can buy any portion of a page measured in column inches. Typically you can specify where you would like the ad to appear (travel, entertainment, sports), but particular ad positions are not guaranteed. Circulation largely determines price.

There are usually discounts for frequent advertisers. Newspapers will often provide preliminary consultation on putting together an ad campaign at no additional cost. Extra charges may be assessed for colour and any staff help provided on artwork, layout, and type setting.

Magazine Advertising

Magazine advertising is a lot like newspaper advertising—flat, one-time rates—with several exceptions. Magazines sell a portion of the page, in full, half, quarter, 1/8, etc. increments. So there are limits on how you use space. Additional charges for preferred positions include the back center spread, inside covers, and those ads placed near popular writers' columns. Normally ads to the magazine are camera-ready, meaning everything is in place to print.

Publisher's statements contain information on circulation, renewal rates, and geographic breakdown of their subscribers. When you consider circulation figures, the primary cost factor, be sure to get a breakdown on paid versus nonpaid circulation. A large percentage of complimentary subscriptions limit your ability to make generalisations about the target audience.

The rise in special interest magazines featuring certain recreation activities and hobbies (such as Canoe), geographic regions (Midwest Living), and lifestyles (Modern Maturity for retired persons) have made it easier to reach distinct market segments. Also consider magazines for the travel trade such as motorcoach tour operators, travel agents, and meeting/convention planners.

Direct Mail Advertising

Direct mail, as the name implies, is a package of advertising materials mailed to selected target market members. Total costs are based on production, list preparation, and mailing activities. Direct mail can appear expensive at first glance, but when you consider the locate one interested customer, it can be a cost-effective strategy. There are print expenses in preparing the information to be which could include letters, brochures, catalogues, postcards, price lists, or coupons. Consider working with a local business, utility company, college, etc., to include paycheck or bill "stuffers" that highlight tourist opportunities.

A mailing list can be purchased: an industry average cost is from $40 to $70 for 1,000 names. It is impossible to overemphasise the importance of the quality of the list you The best list often is previous customers' names obtained from receipts or registers. The informal 20-80 rule in marketing states that 20 percent of your customers are apt to generate 80 percent of your business. They have introduced to the services you provide and can be the most likely prospects. The also can generate good word-of-mouth advertising.

If you mail to the travel trade, keep in mind the volume of mail that travel agents and tour operators receive. Bulk mail costs less than first class postage, but consider many people throw away bulk mail without opening it. The quality of your package can offset this tendency. Try unusual tactics to set your material apart. For example a gift; shop featuring Third Wold handicrafts mailed a letter overseas using colourful stamps of the country to reach previous customers. Include costs for return mail if provide a way for the customer to respond. There is a major time commitment in the mailing itself.

Mailing houses will sort, label, stuff, and tie direct mail packages for a fee. Resorters have been using this idea for years—Christmas letters that remind past guests of great times or to book soon for the upcoming season. The idea is increasing in popularity and has year-round applicability. The community Askov had greater attendance at a local Danish celebration after sending a direct mail piece to members of the Danish-American Society. Lansboro sent out a glossy detailing Christmas activities in town to former guest at lodging establishments. The Winona Chamber of Commerce has mailed a brochure on birdwatching in the region to members of the Audubon Society in the Upper Midwest.

Outdoor Advertising

Billboards are the most common form of outdoor advertising, and can be very effective is used properly. Think of the impact of the Arizona billboards that go up along the freeway near downtown Minneapolis in winter. Conversely, a Minnesota lake scene in downtown Phoenix in August could have a similar effect. Keep the message simple. Billboard strategy is based on size, traffic volume, and type. Most companies that lease advertising prefer at least a two month contract commitment.

Outdoor advertising is usually designed to create awareness. Impulse buying is not common for travel decisions so opportunities to change a traveller's plans are great—with the exception of businesses geared to the travel transit—motels, attractions, gift chops, etc. Instead, your advertising should place the option of a future visit in the mind of the consumer. One campground on Highway 169 North, a major thoroughfare, proclaims "You'd be Here Now if You Had Chosen Us." Similarly, the Minnesota Zoo billboard campaign targets drivers who regularly use Interstate 494 and Highways 7 and 12. Another option to complement media advertising is transit advertising on buses (both inside and outside) and taxis.

Television Advertising

Advertising in prime time evening hours in 15-, 30-, 60- and even 90-second slots is most expensive in television. Match your target market with the characteristics of the people who watch the show. You can scatter television "buys" (purchase of time" across the entire time schedule, or concentrate on specific segments. Some experts advise buying television in weekly increments, contracting for so many spots of specific lengths in specific programmes. Be sure to add on production costs. In major metropolitan areas, advertising agencies often handle television accounts. In smaller markets, you may be able to negotiate directly with the station.

Television is a difficult medium for many tourism industry businesses and destinations with a limited advertising budget. Your ads will be competing for attention with ads that cost hundreds of thousands of dollars to produce, and the quality differences will be noticeable. Your product must also have widespread appeal to be the most effective use of advertising dollars. Think of the flashy summertime commercials several state tourism offices and the Canadian Tourism Board have used on Minnesota stations. Canada has even developed different formats for different markets that the nightlife in the cities or the cultural heritage.

Over 350 cable systems in Minnesota offer more advertising choices. Once cable has been awarded to an area, alternatives include private-for-profit or dedicated channels. You can insert advertising to be seen only by local subscribers on major nationwide channels (for example, ESPN). The recently created Travel Channel offers opportunity to target advertising to an audience inclined to travel. Half of Travel Channel programming is produced in-house, like Arthur Frommer's "Almanac of Travel". The other 50 percent of the air time is allocated of travel packages to viewers and home shopping segments. Again, it is possible to buy local advertising inserts.

Dedicated channels include community-access channels run by organisations such as cities or school districts. These are generally nonprofit entities, so use would be limited to Chambers of Commerce and noncommercial groups. For example, develop a programme on local visitor opportunities to be viewed by hotel guests. You would pay for production costs, but not air time. Some community access channels use a tickertape format to announce upcoming.

Radio Advertising

Radio stations sell time in 10-, 30-, and 60-second blocks. Time on AM stations is during the rush hour traffic to and from work, and mornings. On FM stations, evenings and weekend time slots are most valuable. There are surcharges for placement within special shows such as the morning news, weather or business reports. Radio is a radically different format from print or television, so seek assistance in developing a script that is written for the ear. Ads voiced by well-known personalities can give radio more of a personal touch.

Radio stations have generally been more receptive to tradeouts than other media. This means the station trades air advertising time for a product it receives from you, and often used as a listener prize in radio promotions. For example, a ski resort might trade lift tickets in exchange for its radio spots or a community could offer vacation packages. Attention-getting radio spots can serve diverse purposes. The Lutsen-Tofte area used a three-prong approach, with radio complementing out-of-state print and billboard advertising. Battle Lake designed a last-minute radio blitz to increase attendance at an art festival from local resort guests and residents.

Speciality Advertising

Speciality advertising is used to keep present customers rather than to attract new ones. Gifts with the business or community name, logo, or slogan serve to increase goodwill and remind customers to purchase soon. Calendars, stickers, T-shirts, matchbooks, coffee cups, and posters are in this category. The Explore Minnesota sure packets and soap maintain public awareness of Minnesota as a travel destination.

Miscellaneous Advertising

Consider placing a listing, or ad in the Yellow Pages. Travellers often make accommodation choices from a local phone book. Phone directories for large metropolitan areas are also an option for major lodging facilities and attractions; match your market profile. Mini-attractions such as golf courses and community events can use posters as a way to get information out to visitors they stop or stay—gas stations, resorts, grocery stores, etc.

Advertising Outlets

Two common outlets where a variety of advertising methods are used are trade shows and travel information centers. Trade shows are actually a form of personal selling where you meet with potential customers, but advertising material supports the face-to-face activities. Likewise, travel information centers rely both on one-on-one contact and "take along" advertising pieces. Trade shows are special interest meetings where the general (sports shows) or travel industry representatives convene (American Bus Association for example) to gather information about travel destinations and businesses.

In evaluating this advertising option, include exhibit fees, travel, and per diem expenses, as well as literature costs as direct expenditures. The challenge is to select display literature and giveaway materials to be cost-effective. One way to control costs might be to hand out request cards returned by mail in order to receive expensive promotional pieces. Public travel information centers display community and regional tourism brochures. Check with their staff about the type of inquiries they receive before sending large quantities.

At the local level, many visitor centers will also display materials for private businesses that are members of an association. Long-range plans for some centers include use of video technology. There are also private firms that contract to do private advertising displays at travel information centers, rest stops and airports. Arrangements include backlit panels, unmanned kiosks, and phone boards with toll-free phones. Community cooperative ads are also available to smaller towns. Private sector businesses advertise on one panel, with a "free space" for a nonprofit community attraction. Contact account representatives with these companies for further information.

5

Quality Service Marketing

Most new jobs are created in the service sector, and the growth in the hospitality and tourism industry is a major contributor. Until the mid-1980s, the emphasis within the marketing community was on products. Now services have surpassed products and have taken on a more important role in marketing. Services, such as those offered by providers in the hospitality and tourism industry, have developed marketing strategies and practices that are unique. It has been established that the strategies, tactics, and practices that have been used successfully for product marketers do not always work successfully for those who market services. With the distinct differences between products and services in mind, the field of services marketing has evolved.

Unlike products, which are tangible, services are usually intangible. A service is not a physical good; rather, it is the performance of an act or a deed. This performance often requires consumers to be present during the production or delivery of the service. Service industries, including hospitality and tourism, are actually selling consumers an experience.

Services have been defined to "include all economic activities whose output is not a physical product or construction, is generally consumed at the time it is produced, and provides added value in forms (such as convenience, amusement, timeliness, comfort or health) that are essentially intangible concerns of its first purchaser." Service employees such as front desk agents, housekeepers, hostesses, wait staff, car rental agents, flight attendants, and travel agents are responsible for creating positive experiences for customers. These frontline employees are critical to the success of service firms and play boundary-spanning roles because of their direct contact with customers. These roles are important because customers' perceptions of service firms are formed as a result of their dealings with the boundary-spanning employees.

Growth of Service Marketing

Several reasons underlie the remarkable growth in services.

Changing Patterns of Government Regulation

The reduction in government regulation has spurred the growth of services. In recent years, there has been a very noticeable shift toward the government taking a much less active role in the regulation of business activities. The most noteworthy of these shifts have been in the airline, trucking, telecommunication, and electrical generation and distribution industries. All of these industries have seen significant changes, as the barriers to entry have been removed and regulations governing such marketing elements as price have also been relaxed or entirely removed.

Relaxation of Professional Association Restrictions on Marketing

A new element of competition has been introduced into professions such as law and medicine as more of the practitioners in these areas advertise their services. Bans or restrictions on promotion have been largely removed. Within the hospitality and tourism industry, standards have also changed. We have seen an increase in advertising focusing on direct comparisons, or attacks, on competitors' products and services. This type of advertising strategy creates, or sustains, the perception of superiority in the mind of the consumer in favor of the brand being advertised.

Privatisation of Some Public and Nonprofit Services

The term privatisation was first used in Great Britain when the government adopted the policy of returning national industries from government to private ownership. This transformation has resulted in a greater emphasis on cost containment and a clearer focus on customers' needs. Later, in Central and Eastern Europe, following the fall of communism, we witnessed a continuing transformation from planned or government-run economies to market-driven economies fueled by private companies. Many of these countries' governments have released the control of airlines and travel agencies to private firms.

Technological Innovation

Technology continues to alter the way firms do business and interact with consumers. In all types of businesses, consumers take a more active role in the service delivery process. For example, airlines, in an effort to reduce labour costs and increase speed of service to customers, have aggressively promoted self-check-in, both at the ticket counter and through their Web sites prior to arrival at the airport. Customers print boarding passes, receipts, and other documents without intervention by an airline employee. Express checkout for hotel guests has been in place for many years, but hotel chains continue to experiment with ways to enhance the service, thereby reducing labour costs and/or increasing the customers' perceived value. In other settings, touch-screen computers collect feedback from guests, in much the same manner that comment cards have been used previously.

The ease with which a company can maintain and access a database has permitted the development of sophisticated reservation systems and has led to more sophisticated frequent traveler programmes. The use of more sophisticated reservations and property management systems has allowed hospitality and tourism firms to improve the level of service provided to guests. Guest history data serve as another example of how a hospitality organisation can use technology to gain a competitive advantage. If a hotel guest requests a specific type of pillow, staff can record this preference within the individual's guest history file. When this guest checks into another hotel operated by the chain, the items that were previously requested can be waiting, without the guest even having to request them.

Growth in Service Chains and Franchise Networks

Much of the growth in service firms, including the hospitality industry, has been the direct result of franchising efforts by some of the major companies. Franchising represents a contractual arrangement whereby one firm (the franchisor) licenses a number of other firms (the franchisees) to use the franchisor's name and business practices. Notable lodging organisations such as Choice Hotels International and Marriott International, as well as food service firms such as McDonald's, Burger King, Taco Bell, and Wendy's, have all used franchising as a major vehicle for growth. The continued growth of the hospitality industry by means of franchising has put additional stress on independent owners and operators. In fact, each year the percentage of hospitality and tourism operations that are independently operated decreases.

Internationalisation and Globalisation

Increasing shareholder value often remains directly associated with increasing company sales and profits, and globalisation is one means of achieving this. As more and more of the prime locations are developed domestically, companies look internationally for expansion opportunities. This has been particularly true for fast-food franchisors: a significant proportion of their expansion during the last few years has occurred outside of their traditional domestic markets.

Pressures to Improve Productivity

In many industries within the service economy, competition stays very intense. This factor, when combined with the pressure from investors for higher returns on capital, has resulted in pressure to increase productivity and reduce costs. In many cases, managers seek to reduce labour costs by running leaner operations or using technology to replace humans for some tasks. An example of this was when Delta Airlines encouraged passengers to check in via the Internet, thereby reducing the number of passengers who wanted to check in at the airport. They offered an incentive of 1,000 extra frequent-flyer miles to any passenger who used this service. While increasing productivity and profits remains a highly desirable goal, it must not be done at the expense of longterm customer satisfaction. Without long-term satisfaction, future profitability may exist in jeopardy.

Service Quality Movement

With the advent of consumerism, the public's perception is that service quality has declined. In response, successful firms are using the customer's perception of quality to set performance standards, rather than relying solely on operationally defined standards for service quality. They often conduct extensive research to determine the key elements that impact the customer's perception of service quality. When Ritz-Carlton won the Malcolm Baldrige National Quality Award, this was tangible evidence that paying careful attention to customers' service expectations can have a dramatic impact on the firm.

Expansion of Leasing and Rental Businesses

The expansion of businesses that lease equipment and personnel to firms has been a contributing factor in the growth of the service sector. More and more firms are looking to outsource some elements of their operation, and they often start with elements that are not part of the firm's core product or business. For example, most hotels that host meetings and conventions have outsourced the servicing of the audiovisual needs of groups to a company that specialises in that type of business. The company in turn leases the audiovisual equipment to groups that are holding meetings in the hotel. The company is able to provide more up-to-date and specialised equipment to groups than the hotel might if it provided the service itself. The hotel does not have to maintain an inventory of equipment, and therefore capital costs are reduced.

Manufacturers as Service Providers

Some of the firms that traditionally manufactured and distributed tangible products have found it profitable to provide services as well. For example, most automobile manufacturers have consumer credit agencies to facilitate the leasing and purchasing of automobiles. In the hospitality industry, PepsiCo decided to enter the restaurant industry and distribute its products through acquisitions such as Taco Bell and KFC, but the company later reconsidered this strategy and sold these brands to

Yum! Brands, Inc. In the computer industry, firms such as IBM and Hewlett-Packard provide services in addition to hardware and software. In most cases, the profit margins on services are higher than on products, contributing significantly to the bottom line of the firm.

Pressures on public and nonprofit organisations to find new income sources. All organisations are under pressure to increase sales, which often becomes difficult within the traditional products that a firm sells. There are many reasons for this, but increasing competition and mature industries are often contributing factors. In an effort to find new sources of income, firms often seek new services that will generate new net sales, without cannibalising sales of existing products. For example, a limousine company might expand its city tour business in addition to the other services offered.

Hiring and promotion of innovative managers. In the past, managers in the service industries often spent their entire careers within a single industry, or perhaps even with the same firm. This situation no longer re mains the same, especially at the corporate level of management. Firms often hire individuals from other industries to provide a fresh perspective and fresh ideas. The results can become dramatic. One such individual is Steven Bollenback, president and CEO of Hilton Hotels. Prior to his very positive impact on Hilton Hotels, he had engineered innovative financing at both Marriott International and Trump Hotels and Resorts.

Differences Between Goods and Services

Along with the growth in services, an appreciation for the ways in which services are different from products has developed. The traditional ways of marketing tangible products are not equally effective in services marketing. In many industries, marketing involves tangible manufactured products, such as automobiles, washing machines, and clothing, whereas service industries focus on intangible products such as travel and foodservice. However, before we can explore how services get successfully marketed, we need to examine the ways services differ from products. Lovelock and Wright have identified nine key differences.

— *No ownership by customers.* A customer does not take ownership when purchasing a service. There is no transfer of assets.

— *Service products as intangible performers.* The value of owning a highperformance car or the latest computer lies in the physical characteristics of the product and to some extent the brand image it conveys. The value of purchasing services lies in the nature of the performance. For example, if you decide to celebrate a birthday or anniversary by dining at an expensive restaurant, the value lies in the way in which the service actors perform. When servers come to the table and present all the entrees simultaneously, the choreographed presentation appears in the same manner as a choreographed play or performance.

— *Greater involvement of customers in the production process.* Because consumers tend to be present when receiving service within a hospitality operation, they remain involved in the service production. In many instances, they are directly involved through the element of self-service. Examples of this can be seen in fast-food restaurants as well as in hotels that provide automated check-in and checkout by means of either a machine or a video connection through the television. Airlines have greatly expanded self-service within their operations as a means of reducing labour costs. In any case, the customer's level of satisfaction depends on the nature of the interaction with the service provider, the nature of the physical facilities in which the service gets provided, and the nature of the interaction with other guests present in the facility at the time the service is provided.

— *People as part of the product.* People or firms that purchase services come in contact with other consumers as well as the service employees. For example, a hotel guest waits in line at the front desk or the concierge desk with other guests. In addition, the guests share facilities such as the pool, the restaurant, and the fitness center. Therefore, service firms must also manage consumer interactions to the best of their abilities to ensure customer satisfaction. For example, a hotel's sales office would not want to book group business with a nondrinking religious group at the same time as a reunion of military veterans. The two groups are significantly different in behaviour, and the expectation is that they would not mix well within the facilities at the same time. Similarly, restaurants separate smokers and nonsmokers, and they should try to separate other patrons that show some potential for conflict.

— *Greater variability in operational inputs and outputs.* In a manufacturing setting, the operational production can be controlled very carefully. For example, staff carefully manage inventory and precisely calculate production times. Services, however, are delivered in real time, with many variables not being fully under the control of managers. For example, if a guest has been promised an early check-in but all of the guests from the preceding night are late in checking out, it becomes more difficult for the hotel to honor the arriving guest's request. A service setting remains a more difficult site in which to control quality and offer a consistent service experience. Service firms try to minimise the amount of variability between service encounters, but much of the final product stays situational. There are many uncontrollable aspects of the delivery process, such as weather, the number of consumers present, the attitudes of the consumers, and the attitudes of the employees. Therefore, it becomes impossible to consistently control the quality for services in the same manner as the quality of manufactured products.

— *Harder for consumers to evaluate.* Consumers can receive considerable information regarding the purchase of products; however, they often do not obtain it for services. Prior to buying a product, a consumer can research the product attributes and performance and use this information when making a purchase decision, especially an important one.

— *No inventories for services.* Due to the intangible nature of services, they cannot be inventoried for future use. Therefore, a lost sale can never be recaptured. When a seat remains empty on a flight, a hotel room stays vacant, or a table stays unoccupied in a restaurant, the potential revenue for these services at that point in time becomes lost forever. In other words, services are perishable, much like produce in a supermarket or items in a bakery. It remains critical for hospitality and tourism firms to manage supply and demand in an attempt to minimise unused capacity. For example, restaurants offer early-bird specials and airlines offer deeply discounted fares in an attempt to shift demand from peak periods to nonpeak periods, thereby increasing revenue and profits.

— *Importance of time.* Hospitality services are generally produced and consumed simultaneously, unlike tangible products, which are manufactured, inventoried, and then sold at a later date. Customers must be present to receive the service. There are real limits to the amount of time that customers are willing to wait to receive service. Service firms study the phenomenon of service queues, or the maximum amount of time a customer will wait for a service before it has a significant (negative) impact on his or her perception of service quality. Airline companies offer curbside check-in for the most time-conscious passengers, and restaurants have devised practices such as providing guests with pagers and expanding the bar area in order to reduce the negative effect that results from waiting for service.

— *Different distribution channels.* The distribution channel for services is usually more direct than the traditional channel (i.e., manufacturer-wholesalerretailer-consumer) used by many product firms. The simultaneous production and consumption normally associated with service delivery limits the use of intermediaries. The service firm usually comprises both the manufacturer and the retailer, with no need for a wholesaler to inventory its products. Consumers are present to consume the meals prepared in a restaurant, to take advantage of the amenities in a hotel, and to travel between cities by plane.

Search, Experience, and Credence Qualities

When consumers make purchase decisions, they move through a series of steps that explain the thought process leading up to and following the purchase of a product or service. Prior to making a purchase decision, consumers look for information about the product or service. Search qualities are attributes that the consumer can investigate prior to making a purchase. When purchasing hospitality and tourism services, consumers rely heavily on word of mouth and on promotional elements such as advertising and publicity.

Since services are intangible, search qualities can be difficult to evaluate. However, advances in technology and the increase in consumer advocacy groups have resulted in more information being available to consumers prior to purchase. The second set of qualities consumers use to evaluate services are experience qualities. These refer to the attributes that can be evaluated only after the purchase and consumption of a service. The intangible nature of services forces consumers to rely heavily on experience qualities in the final evaluation of services.

Therefore, a high risk remains associated with the purchase of services. For example, consumers who want to purchase an automobile will test-drive the car and review and consult the consumer performance data that are available on that model. Conversely, consumers who rent cars cannot evaluate their purchases until after they have committed their payment. Few consumers will take the time or make the effort to test-drive potential rental cars prior to mak ing a decision at the time of rental. Similarly, consumers are taking a risk when they choose a restaurant because they cannot sample meals before they are purchased.

Finally, credence qualities are those attributes that are difficult to evaluate even after the service is consumed. Even though you arrive safely at your destination after a flight, you cannot evaluate the pilot's work in any real depth. In many cases, you know a service was not performed correctly only when an obvious mistake exists. For example, bacteria often appear on food served in restaurants, but the public becomes aware of it only when major ramifications such as food poisoning or deaths get publicised. Purchase decisions related to services are more difficult to make because of the lack of search qualities and the difficulty in evaluating credence qualities.

Consumers tend to rely on their own past experiences and those of others when making purchase decisions. Therefore, service firms must obtain as much feedback from consumers as possible. If consumers do not return, the firm may not know why, and the consumers will probably tell others about their experience. Service firms should know if consumers are not satisfied so that appropriate actions can be taken to improve the quality of service and increase repeat business.

Service Quality

Firms use two basic strategies to compete: become a low-cost provider of a particular service and focus on price competition, or focus on quality and try to differentiate your service from those offered by your competitors. Firms that can project high-quality images can charge higher prices. Service quality is a perception resulting from attitudes formed by customers' long-term, overall evaluations of performance. Service quality is affected by all of the individuals who have contact with customers. If one employee provides below-standard service or fails to satisfy the customer, a negative experience could result. Therefore, it is important to understand the entire process of service delivery that leads to consumer perceptions of quality.

Service Quality Process

The service quality process is the product of the expectations and perceptions of a firm's management, its employees, and the customers it serves (Figure 1).

Whenever there are differences in expectations or perceptions between the people involved in the delivery and the consumption of services, a potential for a gap in service quality exists. Firms should diagnose any service quality gaps because there is a direct relationship between service quality and customer satisfaction. Simply stated, when customers are satisfied, they are much more likely to purchase from the service provider again. Over time, if they remain satisfied, they become loyal customers.

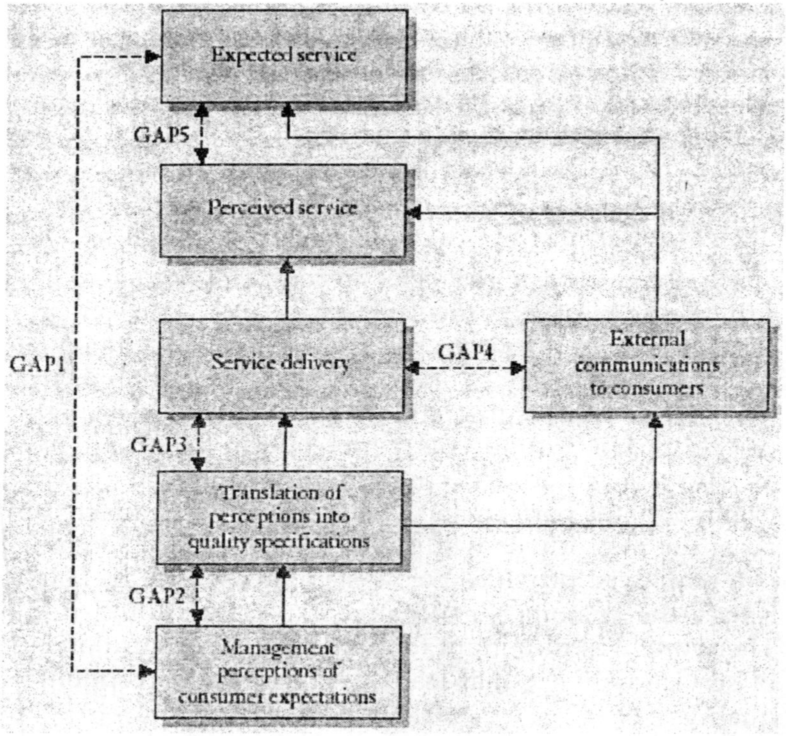

Figure 1. Service quality process

The service gap is the final gap that exists when there is a difference between customers' expectations of a service and their perceptions of the actual service once it is consumed. When this difference occurs, it is the result of one or more gaps that occur earlier in the service quality process. The first potential gap is referred to as the knowledge gap, which occurs when management's perception of what consumers expect is different from the consumers' actual expectations. This gap may lead to other gaps in the service quality process, and it is usually the result of a failure in the firm's research programme or organisational structure.

Firms need to obtain feedback from customers and employees that can be used to design services that will appeal to customers. If the current service offering is not satisfying customers, then the firm should know from its customer surveys or because its employees are willing, and able, to provide valuable information that they obtain from customers, either voluntarily or involuntarily. The second potential gap is referred to as the standards gap, which refers to the discrepancy that can occur between management's perception of what customers expect and how the service delivery process is designed to meet those expectations.

Management establishes the specifications to provide the desired service at the desired level of quality. Therefore, even if management remains accurate in its perception of customer expectations, a gap could still exist in service because the delivery process does not accomplish the goals of the firm. For example, management may have correctly determined the amount of time that customers are willing to wait to check in to a hotel, but they may not schedule enough front desk clerks to meet the customers' expectations. This could result from a lack of commitment on the part of man-agement or the result of management trying to reduce the firm's operating costs.

One of the techniques used by management is to develop a service blueprint -a flow chart that details the delivery process, including the points of contact with customers. This will help to uncover any shortcomings in the delivery process that may lead to a gap in service quality. Management should document each step in the process to identify areas for improvement. The third potential gap is referred to as the delivery gap, which occurs when there is a difference between the service delivery specifications and the actual service delivery.

Management may have correctly assessed customer expectations and developed specifications that will meet these expectations, but employees may not deliver the service properly. For example, a restaurant may specify that wait staff should approach customers within two minutes of seating. However, the wait staff may stand around discussing their plans for later in the evening and ignoring the specifications. Firms must find ways to create an atmosphere for employees that ensures their willingness to perform the job tasks as desired by management.

Employee selection and training are critical in this process, as are the rewards and recognition provided for good performance. The fourth potential gap is referred to as the communications gap, which occurs when there is a difference between the service delivered and the ser vice promised through the firm's external communications with customers. Many firms have a tendency to promise more than they can deliver in an attempt to persuade customers. For instance, advertisements for hospitality and tourism firms lead customers to believe that in the event of a problem or mishap the firms will do whatever they can to satisfy customers.

Making promises to consumers that cannot be delivered is a big mistake that service providers often make. It results in service performance levels that are below consumer expectations, leading to dissatisfaction. Each individual consumer makes purchase decisions and has established, based on past experiences, a set of expectations for the performance of a product or service. Anyone who travels on a regular basis can provide stories related to experiences with airlines, hotels, and restaurants.

Ironically, firms that advertise 100 percent satisfaction guarantees are banking on the fact that most customers will not complain or force the issue. In other cases, firms simply neglect to inform customers about procedures or policies that would affect their expectations. For example, a good waitress will make sure that customers know that a dish is spicy or that a certain entrée will take longer to properly prepare, so that customers can make informed decisions and are less likely to become dissatisfied, because the actual performance will more closely match consumer expectations.

If any of the first four gaps occur, then the service gap will occur because the actual service will not meet the customer's expectations. Comment cards and basic surveys will often uncover a service gap, but they may lack the detail needed to evaluate the other potential gaps. Therefore, firms should have a mechanism in place to obtain feedback from customers and employees that can be used to examine the entire service quality process. If services do not meet customers' expectations of quality, then the customers become dissatisfied and will likely not return. Also, they will convey these negative experiences to their friends and colleagues.

Service Quality Management

To provide high-quality service, all members of the staff, from the highest to the lowest level on the organisational chart, must view the guest as the highest priority. Delivering high-quality service is based on an attitude of serving customers. For example, the mission statement of The Greenbrier, a well-known resort, states, "We are ladies and gentlemen serving ladies and gentlemen." Developing an attitude that places the customer as the highest priority for the business remains critical. Without satisfied customers and repeat patron-age, the business will not succeed in the long term. To develop a servicequality orientation, customers should be perceived in the following way:

— Each customer is the most important person in any business.

— Customers are not dependent on us, but we are dependent on them.

— Customers do not interrupt our work. They are the purpose for it.
— Customers do us a favor when they call. We are not doing them favors by providing them services.
— Customers are part of our business, not outsiders.
— Customers are human beings like us, with the same feelings and emotions.
— Customers bring us their wants, and it is our job to fulfill them.
— Customers deserve the most courteous and attentive service we can provide.
— Customers are the lifeblood of every business.

Firms that use a customer orientation become more successful at providing products and services that meet customers' needs and expectations. In contrast, firms that assume they know what is best for the customer are more likely to fail. This is further illustrated by those firms that successfully engage in relationship and internal marketing.

Relationship Marketing

All progressive companies devote marketing resources to attract and retain new customers. Relationship marketing is based on the proposition that it is less expensive to keep the customers you already have than to acquire new customers. It is shortsighted to think that merely attracting new customers will keep the business headed in a successful direction. Rather, an equal amount of attention and resources should be devoted to keeping the customer base that already exists. In times of slow market growth and increasing competition, it will be less expensive to maintain an existing customer base than to seek new customers.

Relationship marketing involves attracting, developing, and retaining customer relationships. This long-term view toward the customer must be seen as being equal in importance to attracting new customers. Many firms make the mistake of focusing on new customers at the expense of existing customers, and the level of service quality diminishes. For example, hotel sales managers are expected to develop new accounts with corporate and association groups. Sometimes they spend so much time trying to get these new accounts that they neglect some of their existing accounts. This lack of attention may cost the hotel the group's future business because they took the customer for granted. Service firms should build relationships and maintain them. A relationship marketing approach is highly desirable upon meeting the following conditions:

— A customer has an ongoing or periodic desire for the service.

— The service customer controls the selection of the service organisation.

— Alternative service providers make it easy for customers to switch.

All three of these conditions are present in the hospitality and tourism industry. Many firms offer special prices and additional services to highly desirable customers in an attempt to build long-term relationships. These practices are most commonly used with business accounts and frequent users. For example, hotels provide contract rates for corporations that supply a high volume of annual business. Airlines receive one of the lowest rates possible in hotels near airports because they have flight crews who need guest rooms on a daily basis. Also, airlines build relationships with frequent flyers by providing them with additional services such as preboarding, free upgrades, and airport clubs where they can rest or conduct business away from crowded lounges at departure gates.

Internal Marketing

Internal marketing encompasses all activities used by a firm in an effort to improve the marketing effectiveness of its employees. Efforts should be made to communicate with all employees, especially those in boundaryspanning roles who come in contact with customers. The ability to deliver consistent, high-quality service depends on the organisation's ability to recruit, train, retain, and motivate dedicated service personnel.

First, service firms need to select and hire employees who are willing and able to provide high-quality service. There are many people in the job market, and firms need to create attractive positions that appeal to highly motivated individuals. A range of potential service exists that an employee can provide from the minimum necessary to retain the position and not be penalised to the maximum possible service. This variability in the level of possible service is referred to as discretionary effort. For example, if an airline passenger leaves a carry-on item on a flight, the airline's personnel have some discretion as to the level of service they will provide. They can take their time and forward the item to the traveler's next destination, or they can try to deliver it to the traveler before he or she boards the next plane or leaves the airport.

Second, service firms should provide employees with adequate training so they possess the skills that are required in performing their job tasks. In addition, the firm should communicate with employees so they are aware of changes within the organisation as well as upcoming events. If service personnel are well trained and they understand what management expects, the environment is right for success. Firms can use both internal communications, such as newsletters and e-mail, and external communications, such as advertising and public relations, to convey their expectations to employees.

An advertisement can be used to create and manage consumer perceptions and expectations, but at the same time, the ad can be used to educate employees as well. One of the major airlines aired a commercial on television that showed an athletic employee running through the airport to catch a traveler who left his briefcase at the check-in counter. This commercial served two purposes: (1) it let customers know that the airline provided high-quality service, and (2) it gave employees an idea of the firm's service expectations. Finally, firms need to provide employees with rewards and recognition when they perform at a high level of discretionary effort. This motivates service providers to continue performing at high levels and to remain loyal to the firm. Retaining good employees is important in providing high-quality service, and it reduces the costs associated with turnover. It takes a great deal of time and effort to hire and train good employees.

Firms can use extrinsic rewards such as salary increases and bonuses or intrinsic rewards such as recognition and job satisfaction to motivate employees. Many firms recognise "employees of the month" by honoring them with plaques displayed where customers can see them or allowing them to use special parking spaces close to the building.

Importance of Customer Satisfaction

Most firms understand the importance of customer satisfaction and will provide basic training to their employees. The more sophisticated firms actually have instruments that they use to measure customer satisfaction and establish benchmarks for future comparisons. Benchmarking is a process whereby a firm establishes a level of performance by comparing current performance against past performance, or by comparing current performance against the performance of other companies or an entire industry. Data are used to create benchmarks, which then become the standard against which current and future performance is evaluated. Unfortunately, many firms still only pay lip service to customer satisfaction and the complaints received from customers.

Customers who have their complaints resolved to their satisfaction tell an average of 5 people about the experience. These statistics support the contention that a dissatisfied customer tells people about a bad experience more often than a satisfied customer tells people about a good experience. However, firms should take note that it is beneficial to have customers voice their complaints so that they can be resolved and increase the likelihood that the customers will return.

Customer Service and Customer Satisfaction

Improving customer service should be a top priority of all managers working in the hospitality and tourism industry. Customer satisfaction occurs when a firm's service, as perceived by customers, meets or exceeds expectations. Firms that can consistently meet or exceed customer expectations will develop good reputations and often good quality images. When we travel, we encounter service providers in hotels and restaurants who provide exceptional service. This type and consistency of service does not happen by accident; it begins with a commitment by management to make it that way. Conversely, when the opposite occurs, the finger should be pointed at management as well.

There are five-step process for improving customer service:

1. *Define your standards of quality service with measurable indicators*. Before you can evaluate the level of service provided by employees within your organisation, you

must establish the standards by which they will be judged. These standards, or benchmarks, should be observable and measurable. For example, it might be reasonable to expect front desk agents to answer the telephone within four rings or room service to deliver meals within 30 minutes of when the order was received. Once these standards are developed, they must be communicated to all personnel. It remains crucial that standards be clearly defined before any plans are developed to improve the level of service.

Martin suggests two major dimensions to define quality service: the procedural dimension and the convivial dimension. The procedural dimension includes incremental flow of service, timeliness, accommodating consumer needs, anticipating consumer needs before they occur or are requested by the consumer, communicating in a clear and concise manner, obtaining consumer feedback, and coordinating through proper supervision. The convivial dimension includes displaying a positive attitude and body language, using the guest's name as a means of delivering personal attention, attending to the guest on a personal basis, providing guidance to guests who are indecisive, and solving problems that arise.

2. *Assess your current situation.* As in any continuous improvement programme, before you move forward, you must determine your current position. This can be done by objectively assessing the level of service currently provided within the organisation; this involves conducting an audit of the services provided by service personnel within the organisation. As a result of the audit, the strengths and weaknesses of the firm can be determined; this will provide a means of building on the aspects of service that are positive and improving the areas that are deficient. Audits can

be conducted using mystery shoppers, or corporations may use staff members to audit the performance of units within the company.

3. *Develop effective service improvement strategies.* This must be accomplished through well-planned and thorough training of service providers. Attention must be paid to identifying objectives for the training and providing specific instructions and clear descriptions of the expected outcome(s) of the training.
4. *Initiate your solutions carefully.* As with any plan, implementation is the most critical stage. You should proceed with caution, taking steps incrementally rather than all at once. You should build on small successes, rather than trying to accomplish too much too soon.
5. *Provide feedback, recognition, and rewards.* Positive feedback must be provided if the change in behaviour continues. A reward structure must be provided that will maintain the level of interest and enthusiasm among the service providers throughout their careers. This represents a major challenge for management, but one that is well worth the effort. Finally, management must continually evaluate the performance of its employees and make the appropriate changes. Over time, customers' expectations of service firms change, and competitive firms may increase the level of service that is considered the standard in an industry. Therefore, firms must constantly reassess their strategies and redefine their service standards. Service performance and customer satisfaction should be measured and evaluated using benchmarks established during previous periods. Also, direct comparisons with the performance of firms considered industry leaders are an excellent way to establish goals for future improvement.

Service Failures, Customer Complaints, and Recovery Strategies

Service failures occur at critical incidents, or "moments of truth," in the service encounter, when customers interact with a firm's employees. It is important to provide service personnel with the authority and the recovery tools necessary to correct service failures as they occur.

Service Failures

The timeliness and form of response by service providers to service failures will have a direct impact on customer satisfaction and quality perceptions. Service failures are assigned to one of three major categories: (1) responses to service delivery system failures, (2) responses to customer needs and requests, and (3) unprompted and unsolicited employee actions.

The first category, system failures, refers to failures in the core service offering of the firm. These failures are the result of normally available services being unavailable, unreasonably slow service, or some other core service failure that will differ by industry. For example, a hotel's pool may have a leak and be closed, a customer may have to wait a long time for the shuttle to an airport car rental agency, or an airline might mishandle a passenger's luggage.

The second category, customer needs failures, are based on employee responses to customer needs or special requests. These failures come in the form of special needs, customer preferences, customer errors, and disruptive others (i.e., disputes between customers). For example, a hotel guest may want to have a pet in the room, a customer may want to be switched to an aisle seat on an airplane, a customer at an event may lose his ticket, or a customer in a restaurant may be smoking in a nonsmoking section.

The third category, unsolicited employee actions, refers to the actions, both good and bad, of employees that are not expected by customers. These actions can be related to the level of attention an employee gives to customers, to unusual actions that can be performed by employees, to an action's reinforcement of a customer's cultural norms, or to an employee's actions under adverse conditions. For example, a hostess in a restaurant could anticipate the needs of a family with a small child, a hotel front desk clerk could give a free upgrade to a guest who waited in line too long, a flight attendant could ignore passengers with children, or a cruise ship employee could help to evacuate passengers during a crisis.

Customer Complaint Behaviour

Certain undesired outcomes are associated with dissatisfied customers. Two of the most common are to engage in negative word of mouth and to change service providers. A third, less common reaction is to engage in some form of retaliation. This retaliation can range from a negative word-of-mouth campaign to causing physical damage or launching a major protest. The way a firm approaches and handles complaints will determine its long-term performance.

Some firms show a dislike for customers who complain, while other firms create an atmosphere that encourages customers to voice their concerns. For example, Bertucci's Brick Oven Pizzerias, headquartered in Massachusetts, offers customers a tollfree number that they can call to register a complaint. One of the primary reasons for doing this is to provide dissatisfied customers with an outlet to have their concerns heard and to take immediate steps to resolve the complaint. By doing so, the firm hopes to reduce negative word of mouth and to retain customers.

Most customers complain in an attempt to reverse an undesirable state. Other more complicated reasons for complaining are to release pressure, to regain some form of control over a situation, or to get the sympathy of others. Whatever the reason, the outcome is that customers are not completely satisfied, and it is in the firm's best interest to know when this occurs. There are many other dissatisfied customers who do not complain because they don't know what to do or they don't think it will do any good.

Recovery Strategies

When customers complain, firms are presented with the opportunity to recover from service failures. Recovery strategies, and actions occur when a firm's reaction to a service failure results in customer satisfaction and goodwill. In fact, customers who are involved in successful service recoveries often demonstrate higher levels of satisfaction than customers who do not report service failures or complain. The following list describes popular service recovery strategies:

Cost/benefit analysis. Service firms should compare the costs of losing customers and obtaining new customers with the benefits of keeping existing customers. Most firms place a high value on retaining customers. However, some guests take advantage of satisfaction guarantees and complain on every occasion. Many hotel chains, such as Doubletree, maintain a database on complaints and will flag chronic complainers.

Actively encourage complaints. It is better to know when customers are not satisfied so that action can be taken to rectify the situation. It is im-portant to note that while unhappy customers may not complain to service firms, they will often complain to their family and friends. Hospitality and tourism firms use comment cards and toll-free numbers to encourage customers to provide feedback. Also, service personnel are trained to ask customers whether everything was satisfactory.

Anticipate the need for recovery. Service firms should "blueprint" the service delivery process and determine the moments of truth, or critical incidents, where customers interact with employees. The process can be designed to avoid failures, but recovery plans should be established for use in the event that a failure occurs.

Respond quickly. The timelier the response in the event of a service failure, the more likely that recovery efforts will be successful. Once a customer leaves a service establishment, the likelihood of a successful recovery falls dramatically. Based on this principle, firms such as Marriott International provide service hotlines at each hotel to help resolve problems quickly. Managers and associates know that the speed with which they respond is often as critical as what the final resolution becomes.

Train employees. Employees should be informed of the critical incidents and provided with potential strategies for recovery. For example, some hotel training programmes use videotaped scenarios of service failures to show employees potential problems and the appropriate solutions.

Empower the front line. In many cases, a successful recovery will hinge on a frontline employee's ability to take timely action and make a decision. Firms should empower employees to handle service failures at the time they occur, within certain limits. For example, Ritz-Carlton allows its employees to spend up to $1,000 to take care of dissatisfied customers. One of the classic examples of a service failure involved Northwest Airlines during a major winter storm at the Detroit airport. Unfortunately, due to the heavy snow, many outbound flights were canceled, and no gates were available for unloading passengers from the inbound flights. This traffic jam left many passengers stranded as the airplanes sat on the taxiways for as long as eight hours. Northwest's inability to provide the passengers with information or a solution resulted in hundreds of unhappy passengers and a class action lawsuit. Having delayed flights and a shortage of gates is not a new phenomenon at airports in climates such as Detroit's, and Northwest Airlines should have had a viable service recovery programme in place that could have lessened the severity of the problem.

Techniques to Assess Customer Satisfaction

One of the critical components of a firm's commitment to customer satisfaction is feedback that provides an assessment of the firm's performance. Then benchmarks can be established and future progress can be evaluated. Also, these measures can be used to reward service personnel in a way that stays consistent with a firm's customer satisfaction goals. The following section describes the most common techniques used by firms to assess customer satisfaction.

Spoken comments and complaints. Listening to consumer comments and complaints remains the most straightforward way to evaluate customer satisfaction. Service firms should set up formal systems that encourage customer and employee feedback regarding service experiences. Management should not overlook the value of the information obtained by boundary-spanning personnel through their normal contact with customers. One of the most recent approaches is providing toll-free numbers so that customers can call to voice complaints.

Surveys and comment cards. Many hospitality and tourism firms leave comment cards in guest rooms, on tables in restaurants, and at other points of contact so that they can obtain feedback. One of the problems associated with this method is the lack of representation. The response rate is small, and it tends to be biased toward those who are most upset and chronic complainers. Larger operations will conduct surveys through the corporate offices by either telephone or mail. Surveys will normally be more representative than comment cards and provide more detailed information. These types of surveys also provide for a more representative sample of customers.

Number of repeat customers. Service firms can gauge customer satisfaction by keeping track of repeat business. Higher levels of satisfaction would be associated with higher percentages of repeat customers. This models an unobtrusive method of assessing customer satisfaction, but it does not provide much detail.

Trends in sales and market share. Another way to evaluate customer satisfaction without direct contact with customers is to examine the firm's internal sales records. Comparisons can be made on a month-to-month basis and with the same period of the previous year. Higher levels of satisfaction would be associated with increases in sales. However, firms should be careful with this method because there are many possible explanations for increases in sales. For example, the firm may have launched a new advertising campaign, a competitor may be renovating or going out of business, or the firm may have decreased its prices. In addition to examining sales records, firms should also look at market share. This measure considers sales in relation to the competition, which is a more accurate assessment of improved market performance. However, there could also be other explanations for changes in market share besides customer satisfaction.

Shopping reports. Another approach used by hospitality and tourism firms involves having someone consume a service just like any other customer. The "secret shopper" can be an employee of the firm, an outside person chosen by the firm, or an employee of an outside firm that specialises in this service assessment activity. These shoppers are normally equipped with detailed evaluation forms based on company guidelines that can be used to record the desired information. It is often recommended that someone outside the firm be used in an attempt to maintain some level of objectivity. It is important to have a particular operation evaluated by more than one shopper on several occasions throughout the desired period. Doing so will result in a more representative sample of service experiences.

Service trends affecting the hospitality and tourism industry: Identifying trends within any business is one of the keys to success. Being in a position to identify what is occurring and what is likely to occur in the future remains very important. When studying trends in a broad sense, one should examine five major areas: the competitive environment, the economic environment, the political and legal environment, the social environment, and the technological environment. Several issues and trends are critical to understanding hospitality and tourism marketing. They help put into proper perspective what occurs within the competitive marketplace. Three trends that are having an impact on the hospitality industry and will continue to do so are shrinking customer loyalty, increasing customer sophistication, and increasing emphasis on the needs of individual customers.

Decreasing customer loyalty

Advertising and promotion for the hospitality and tourism industry's product-service mix have traditionally focused on the product, the services provided, and the physical plant or atmosphere in which the customer enjoys the product-service mix. Today, many hospitality and tourism firms focus their promotions on price; that is, heavy price competition exists along with a good deal of discounting. Unfortunately, price discounting exists as a short-term strategy that seldom builds brand loyalty. Consumers often shop around for the best deal and are loyal only to organisations that give them a consistently superior one.

Recognising this, companies have sought ways to increase brand loyalty, especially among heavy users of the productservice mix. The best examples of this approach are the frequent flyer programmes promoted by the airlines and the frequent traveler programmes promoted by the lodging companies. These loyalty programmes are commonplace in the lodging industry; all of the major chains use loyalty programmes to encourage and reward frequent guests. The strategy behind loyalty programmes is to hook the customer with points which can be redeemed for products or services. The more frequently the customer stays at a hotel operated by the company, the more points are earned. The basic concepts common to all of these programmes are:

- Identify individuals who frequently purchase your product-service mix.
- Recognise the contribution those individuals make to the success of your company.
- Reward those individuals with awards and incentives that will increase their loyalty to your company and its brands.

Tie-ins with other companies providing travel-related services are also frequently used. For example, airlines, hotels, and car rental companies frequently offer bonus points within their programmes if the traveler uses the services offered by one of the companies participating in the tie-in. Both the airlines and the hotel companies are constantly making minor alterations to their programmes.

Increasing consumer sophistication

The budget segment of the lodging industry has

undergone significant growth in the last several years. This growth has been fueled by the consumer demand for affordable accommodations that provide good value. In fact, consumers focus more on value and less on quality or price alone. Consumers have become more sophisticated and understand the concept of value at any price level. Companies have responded with brands that offer good quality at an affordable price. Each of these brands features nicely appointed guest rooms, limited or no public meeting space, limited or no food service provided on the hotel site, and a complimentary continental breakfast for guests. These limited-service brands incur lower development and operating expenses and thereby can provide guests with a lower price and good value, something that all consumers are seeking.

Hotels in the upscale segment are also trying to increase the consumer's perception of value. They continually provide a broad assortment of amenities, such as health clubs on the property, business centers, rooms that provide more work space for business travelers, and personalised concierge service. These properties are striving to become "one-stop" destinations, providing a complete product-service mix that includes many food and beverage outlets, in-house office services, a wide variety of meeting room configurations, and other services, such as recreation, that will appeal to potential guests.

Within the fast-food service segment, companies often "bundle" their products in an attempt to increase sales and provide a better value for their customers. For example, they combine a sandwich, a large order of french fries, and a large soft drink at a price lower than what the items would cost if purchased separately. Similarly, tour operators and travel agents attempt to provide customers with more value by "bundling" the various components of travel (e.g., airline ticket, hotel room, car rental, and tickets for tourist atservice tractions) at a price lower than the sum of the individual components. This approach is known as product bundling.

Increasing the needs of individual customers

The markets within both hospitality and tourism segments have been segmented for a long time. In the past 5 to 15 years, this trend has become even more pronounced. Mass marketing has become a thing of the past as more firms extend their product lines to meet the specific needs of smaller segments of travelers and diners. This phenomenon has become most apparent in the lodging industry. During the last decade, most of the major lodging chains developed several new brands or types of lodging properties to appeal to market segments that they were not currently serving. In addition, many hotel chains have merged with or acquired other hotel chains that focus on different market segments.

Improvements in technology have given firms the ability to maintain large databases that detail consumer purchasing behaviour and preferences. This information can be used to direct marketing efforts toward individual customers or market segments. Instead of relying on the mass media for promotions, a marketer can target past customers through direct mail and e-mail with special promotions and incentives that have a higher probability of being successful. There is more customisation of products and promotions and less wasted coverage with media campaigns.

6

Technology in Hospitality Marketing

The hospitality industry is in the unenviable position of having to meet guest needs, owner/franchisee demands and employee expectations -all in the face of threats of terrorism, war and economic uncertainties. Guests seek differentiated experiences. Owners seek more timely access to information. Employees seek improvements in guestfacing applications. Yet, most guest-facing technologies do not contain the functionality and integration necessary to support service excellence. They simply have not kept up with the changing demands.

The industry is struggling with a single source of the truth and single image strategies for inventory, guest information and marketing/operational content. How will this evolve? This perspective on the evolution of technology in the hospitality industry advocates a centrally or regionally provisioned architecture to develop an above-property view of strategic property and guestspecific applications.

Hoteliers are forced to simultaneously focus in different directions. Their reactions to these challenges and how effective they are at juggling these factors will ultimately define how well they weather the storm. Key challenges include:

Commoditisation: Brand capital is eroding and hotels are threatened by commoditisation. Guests are becoming savvier-they seek differentiated experiences. The brand is no longer the driving force..increasingly more and more guests are becoming brand agnostic-their perception of limited brand differentiation further exasperates the issue. Guests are increasingly looking for niche offerings and personalised services that are delivered consistently.

Distribution: Relentless rate pressure brought on by rate transparency, online intermediaries and aggressive corporate procurement tactics are compounding the issue. Online intermediaries are driving a wedge between major brands and the brand-agnostic guest. These online channels are often popular with hotel owners who see them as an effective way to move inventory. Some hoteliers are combating this by pushing direct connect strategies to combat the effect in the corporate market, reducing the dependency on the global distribution systems and enabling a one-to-one relationship with the guest.

The industry will rely heavily on a next generation technology architecture to address the challenges hotels are facing at present. This architecture will provide the underlying infrastructure and services that allow hotels to reposition their employees to focus on value-added guest interactions, by automating core transactions and providing consistent access to guest data. It will provide hotels with opportunities to leverage technology advances to improve the guest experience. Technology will be pervasive yet invisible.

Hotels will have the ability to quickly and flexibly innovate and react to market needs, wants and desires. New concept time-to-market will be greatly reduced, aided by adaptive technology. Hotels will standardise back-of-the-house and key front-of-thehouse functions across business units, brands, regions and properties, by placing them on a single technology platform and implementing a common business process and organisational framework. External linkages will become easier-applications will draw on common standards libraries for information interchange among systems.

Complicated, customised interfaces between systems and organisations will be passé. The operational and financial benefits will be enormous-cross-brand employee mobility and training cost reduction are some advantages. A logical move for agile hotel corporations, next generation technology applications will be based around an on-demand technology infrastructure. IT services, applications and data will be available as and when needed.

Hotel companies will be able to provide transactional-based models to their franchisees, owners and individual properties, which will only pay for services availed. Installing applications will involve downloading and running them within a browser window. Hotels will move to a variable cost structure where financial models are based on a per-use concept. Supporting and managing infrastructure that is not fully utilised will be a thing of the past. This will free up much needed capital which hotels can use to focus on their raison d'etre.

The new hospitality technology model will place a greater emphasis on enterprise-wide standards. It will employ adaptable, reusable components that can plug into each other-applications will be easily configurable depending upon business size and scope. This new model will be based around a single image of guest information, inventory and content. Users will see the same data regardless of where they tap into the value chain. Hotels will regain control of distribution by limiting the use of indirect online channels; direct connect strategies in the corporate market will become the norm, rather than the exception.

Application services will be delivered above-property via on-demand solutions. They would include property management, point of sale, sales and catering, HR, back office and financials, resulting in improved services and a reduced technology footprint on property. Advances in network connectivity, reliability and security will allow these applications to be hosted centrally and made available through a browser-based front end. Where connectivity is an issue, local models will be supported-relevant data will be downloaded, used to support business processes, and synched with the central repository the next time network connectivity is made available.

The next generation hospitality technology architecture will bring tremendous benefit to the hospitality industry. An on-demand, aboveproperty delivery of services will reduce IT costs and infrastructure investment at the property level. Standardised applications and a single image of guests, inventory and content will provide a consistent view across all touch points in the value chain. Linkages with external applications and organisations will be handled via common information interchange standards. Hotel management will have access to a common, centralised view of pertinent operational information that will be made available to them via customisable on-demand workplaces. This is an interesting future indeed.

Impact of Globalisation

The travel industry is affected by increased competition through globalisation, diversified customer dcrnands and expectations, as well as growing of computer-based knowledge. On the other hand, it is obvious that exactly the changes caused by globalisation at first and at most affect the inunediate holders of business activities within the travel sector. While thriving to be competitive in the global market, exactly the hospitality industry is exposed and overburdened by exclusively high costs for:

— promotion in the global market,
— inunediatc communication / interactivity with the clients / tourists,
— booking by guests from distant tourist generating destinations,
— market research.

The costs mentioned above can be reduced by usllig WWW in tourism business. Namely, the Internet and its application (WWW) have created information infrastrrrettrrc which now rivals the Plain Old Telephone System (POTS) and other traditional ways ol perfornung business in size, coverage and popularity. However, some authors emphasise the uncertainty of reacting of potential guests from all over the world to the change of information and distribution medium, which is to help them reach desired destination. Individual experts suggested the policy and strategy, which should be adopted by developing countries in order to increase their participation in e-business in tourism, and the possible role of UNCTAD and other international organisations in developing suggested policies and strategies.

Since tourism is the leading world industry at the begiruling of the new millerrniunr, if supported by the Internet it represents the most popular e-business category, i.e. the number one on-line segment. Explosive growth of the online travel market is being expected, and it was estimated to reach $30 billion in 2000. In the enviroment of market-based economy and free trade, tourism in transitional counlires cannot `survive' without entrepreneurship programmes doing business over the Internet, because today this is the only way to become an active participant in the global market. The emerging globalisation and concentration of supply increase the level of competition and require new Internet marketing strategies for destinations.

Role of Internet in Marketing Process

The Internet is the global "network of networks" of interlinked computers operating on a standard protocol which allows data to be transferred between them. As an information exchange system, the most important aspect of the Internet is its connectivity, the ability to allow everyone to access the network. The potential of using the Internet for marketing activities is derived from its general use as an information exchange system in the digital age. The information can be stored, indexed, retrieved, restructured and redistributed automatically by software and without human intervention. The Internet connects companies with companies, companies with customers, and people with people without regard to time, space and hardware/ software platforms.

Although the Internet originated in the 19605, it is only in recent years that it has become a buzz-word. Internet services fall into two broad categories: communication services and information services. Communication services such as e-mail, and e-mail-based discussion lists and net news, allow the direct exchange of information between Internet users. Information services, including Telnet, Gopher and anonymous FTP (the File Transfer Protocol), allow users to access data that has been made available by other users. Since 1993, the Internet has been transformed completely by its newest component the World Wide Web (WWW or the Web). The WWW not only integrates other file transfer protocols like Gopher and FTP, but also allows the user to access hosts through Telnet, read newsgroups and use e-mail. Through an Internet browser, a user can link to any web sites and may explore the Internet resource in an unprecedented way for both leisure and commercial purposes. Moreover, the Web's capability to blend text, pictures, sounds and video clips into multimedia documents played the key role in popularising the Internet beyond its traditionally academic boundaries and become an effective communication means in business and everyday life. Indeed, the WWW has been so successful that it changed the appearance of the Internet and for many it even become synonymous with the Internet itself.

The rapid growth of the Internet, especially the WWW, has attracted a great deal of interest among both academic researchers and business practitioners, especially in the fields of Information Technology (IT) and marketing. There are also an increasing number of publications on Internet tourism marketing, in the last few years. The works of Bender, Sheldon, Inkpen, Richer and O'Neil-Dunne, Buhalis and Schertler, Marcussen and O'Connor, among others, have provided the necessary background and some in-depth discussions of the various issues of marketing tourism on the Internet, in particular its impacts on tourism distribution. However, this field of research is, by and large, still in its infancy and much more effort must be made to improve our understanding of the Internet's role in tourism marketing and the ways through which tourism organisations and destinations can exploit its full potential.

The Internet is widely recognised as an extremely valuable marketing tool. It is generally held that the Internet offers substantial advantages over traditional means of communication: reduced costs of information exchange; increased speed of information transfer and retrieval; increased customer involvement in and control of transactions; and greater flexibility of using the marketing mix. Its main business uses include communications, market research, customer services, market penetration, product development, cost savings through process reengineering, direct marketing, advertising and product delivering.

Internet Application

Although applicable in all business activities, e-business has had the biggest success in the following areas until today:

— e-business
— e-marketing
— e-banking
— e-stock exchange
— e-reservation systems

In the first place, it is necessary to define the difference between the Internet and the World Wide WEB. The Internet is a huge data network that spans most of the globe, linked by an enormous assortment of high-capacity data cables, over thousands of routing locations. Data that travels over the Internet get broken into small pieces, or packets, which get routed to their destination and then reassembled.

Since the majority of given activities make an unavoidable component of doing business in the hospitality industry, it is possible to draw a parallel between traditional way of doing business and on-line way by using the Internet. The latter is becon ung increasingly competitive in terms of:

— providing information
— immediate contact with key service providers,
— immediate feedback to the given information,
— pricing,
— marketing and brand building,

— market research,
— booking / reservation.

However, using the on-line way does not exclude the traditional way, but enables expanding of the group of `old' customers, by reaching new on-line customers and establishing a whole new customer base. Also, UNCTAD, sugestes that new e-tourism channels should be integrated into traditional and non-traditional distribution channels and foster the development of special-interest tourism WEBsites. Therefore, conducting awareness campings about etourism is a special tasks for the hospitality industry.

World Wide Web

Using the WWW for promotion and distribution of tourism products or services to potential consumers became inevitable. The Internet is a medium with the fastest increase of usage and it represents a new dimension in the promotion system in the global market. At the same tinge it is an effective system for competition which enables possibilities to use this direct distribution channel effectively. Tourism and tourism products are ideal for marketing on the Internet, because tourism is an information-intensive industry.

Internet develops a relationship of suppliers and consumers providing them with personalised promotional materials. Tourism organisation can no longer be content to print brochures and catalogues, but it should fiinction by using uniovative range of techniques. Under these new circumstances, traditional marketspace model is broadened by two new elements:

1) Customer Relationships,
2) Technology dimension consisting of two separate elements

— interactivity, and

— connectivity.

Since the customer holding a central position within the marketspace is the priority, the creation of WEB sites must be directed towards him. Customer relationships are located in the central part of the marketspace model, and they point to an individual customer related marketing. There is also a growing realisation among corporations that the Internet has forever charred the traditional paradigm of marketing and remote customer contact.

The days of mass marketing and remote customer contact are gone. Interactivity designates intense relationships between an enterprise and customers, and creates new paradigms for product design and customer service. Connectivity refers to creation of a shared global marketplace.

The radical growth of connectivity is giving rise to new conununication and coordination mechanisms linking organisations to their customers, as well as fostering greater communication between the customers themselves. In order to achieve the most effective connectivity, the WEB sites must be provided with the following links:

a) links leading from a selected destination to diverse offer items (including for example: accommodation, heritage, restaurants, events etc.),

b) links from already selected WEB site to other checked offer items within the destination.

In this way the service provider leads the WEB customer through diversified offer within this destination by recommending checked links on his own WEB site. Therefore, the WEB site of tourism enterprise has the effect of a marketing tool of both its own service or product and of the service or products of all other through links promoted enterprises.

Intemet-based Reservation Systems

One of the major uses of the Internet is the development of Intemet-based reservation systems. They date back to the period when they were primarily used by air-line companies, but aflerwards they were transformed into multi-users systems without which it would be impossible for other transport companies, travel and hospitality organisations to function.

The enterprises in the hospitality indsutry have got two possibilities - either to use some of electronic advertisers of supply and demand as a means of sale and reservation of the services or to stay oriented only to the WEB site. In the both mentioned cases the WEB site is a means of both promotion and reservation.

While developing and implementing WEB reservation concept, the hospitality industry can use enormous advantages over the traditional reservation chaimels. In this way it has a possibility to offer automated payment, immediate access to valid price and availability of current information. In addition, this means reduction of steps a customer has to undertake while booking in traditional way, and consequently significant cost saving. The Internet also takes supportive role in conducting all transactions, some of them being: information, reservation, booking, payments, etc.

Today, the acceptance of this new model of reservation in the hospitality industry is increasing. Out of the total number of WEB sites, which was estimated 116.000 in 1999, according to some authors' assertions only 6%, i.e. 6500 offered the ability to execute transactions online.

It is already estimated that by year 2003 over 30% of online sales will be generated by on-line travel alone, including actual travel products as well as advertising earned by travel-oriented sites. UNCTAD sugestes that in order to build trust and consumer confidence and to ensure privacy and the protection of consumers and intellectual property rights, appropriate laws and regulations and service standards should be established. Moreover, hospitality industry employees should cooperate in setting up an international framework to protect travellers conducting transactions on the Internet.

Internet as Market Research Tool

In order to gain competitive position in the tourism market it is indisputable that Internet-based market research is necessary for finding the ways of adapting to the needs of on-line tourism service users. However, in contrast to traditional market reserach, if using the Internet as a medium for research, there is a possibility to get high qulity infomnation, with less costs and quite fast.

UNCTAD suggests that available research on e-commerce should be reviewed, and additional research conducted when necessary, in order to provide information on market trends, consumer needs, WEBsite use, demographic profiles and the impact of non-availability of on-line payments and other information that may support the development of a sustainable hospitality industry. A possible classification of internet based reserach is based on respodent's point of view' and is as follows:

1. *E-mail survey* - this is the oldest and the simpliest way of conducting research; a parallel to traditional mail surveys can be drawn.
2. *News-groups survey* - this kind of reserach is based on sin ular topic entities on the basis of which the reserach is being conducted and having as a consequence relatively small sample size.

3. *WEB based survey* - this is the most corrnrron way of the three. It represents a tremendeous potential for the market reserach experts, offering them a tool for fast and cheap reserach, generating more accurate information.

A prerequisite for a quality based research are high quality standards including sophisticated probability sampling, precise project control, rigorous quality control procedures, advanced questionnaire programming, and insightful analysis. Since WEB based surveys represent a growing segment of Internet research, the benefits of conducting them should be mentioned as divided in four different categories according to their characteristics:

1) inexpensive,
2) response speed,
3) overall effectiveness, and
4) its visual appeal.

However, certain problems should be taken into consideration. Dahlen, divides them in five categories:

1) self-selection,
2) unequal probabilities of sample inclusion,
3) unknown response rate,
4) not being noticed by people and
5) unnecessarily low response rates.

Although still in phase of development, WEB surveys are becornalg increasingly used by many tourism enterprises as significant tool for conducting market research. In a broader context, the technological improvement will affect the percentage of the population using the Internet. This will directly lead to the possibilitiy to sample the general population. All of thus will enable broad applicability of Internet research i11 the hospitality industry.

Email Marketing

Email marketing is a crucial component of the hotel eMarketing and online distribution strategy. The shift toward online purchasing suggests that the website is becoming a key point of entry to establish interactive relationship with your customers and capture client email profiles. Over 192 million North Americans are active Internet users (Nielsen) and 37 million of them have already purchased travel online. The Internet offers a vast, interactive, content-rich media and most importantly, a growing distribution channel for the hospitality market. It is estimated that 8%-10% of all hotel bookings will originate on the Internet in 2002. In fact, some hotels already generate 20%-30% of their total bookings from the Internet.

Email gets the most attention of any hospitality eMarketing effort because intuitively it makes sense—since email can create direct revenue opportunities with past, present, and future customers. Email marketing increases revenue opportunities throughout each customer's purchasing life cycle. The reason this is effective is because a total email marketing strategy addresses the entire buying process from initial email capture to message evaluation and everything in between including copy creation, type of messaging, follow-up, and vendor partnership, all components of a comprehensive communications strategy Once the strategy is built, an effective email campaign serves as a powerful sales force and marketing channel.

Why a total email marketing strategy in hospitality makes competitive sense:

— Serves both as direct-response vehicle and branding tool

— Creates personalised interactive relationships with customers

— Targets and entices recipients with relevant promotions

— Plants seed in the minds of recipients regarding future travel plans

— Serves as a tool to move distressed inventory

— Functions as a sales force – tens of thousands reached in seconds

— Recruits and retains customers, new and old

— Least expensive form of active marketing available

Today, everyone uses email. We read, forward, file, and print email. We send email to friends, family, and clients. Furthermore, almost everybody has at one time or another actively signed up to receive travel related information from a travel supplier or third-party collection service. Travel is a sought after product and a top information category chosen by most Internet users.

The Aberdeen Group indicates that email marketing has grown more than 270% from 1999 to 2000 and rapid growth is expected to continue well into 2005. An estimated 30 billion permission-based email messages were sent in 2001; a number that will grow to 150 billion in 2005.

By category, travel related email marketing retains a loyal audience, especially if it offers the recipient value, accurate communication, relevance, and familiarity. Forrester Research points out that on average, only 5 percent of recipients have ever unsubscribed from any travel related list. Indeed, some travel-related email campaigns report response rates as high as 25%. Let's face it; consumers want to learn about travel specials and promotions. Even travel agents serve as a viable audience as they too seek bookable opportunities.

Thanks to technology and the law, filtering agents and anti-spam laws have begun reigning-in annoying junk email. Filtering products such as Spamex and Spamcop, which cost less than $30 off the shelf, delete messages sent by anonymous senders to group lists and can filter by key words in the message itself.

Permission-based Email Marketing

Permission-based email marketing is the second-generation email approach that goes well beyond guerilla email marketing, known as email spam. A permission-based customer list is one in which you asked the customer permission to enter personal information voluntarily including an email address for the purpose of marketing, i.e. you obtain "permission" to send promotional emails. Opt-in or opt-out options enable the user to sign up or be removed from a marketing list. Growth in permission-based, 100% opt-in, opt-out practices consistently cleanse the customer lists to produce the most robust client lists possible. Once a firm starts an email collection process, it should include these features resulting in email that will be opened and read time and again without concern of violating email privacy norms.

Precision e-mail marketing is the next, third generation email approach that dynamically "reads" customer profiles, purchasing habits and history to create highly personalised emails. Over the past year airlines have used this type of marketing extensively to promote special offers in order to sell seats. Actually, permission based email and precision email marketing have become the airlines' preferred marketing tool. Why? It is cheap and it works! For example, precision e-mail marketing has generated up to a fivefold increase in response rates and tenfold lower conversion costs than direct mail (IMT Strategies).

Why does email marketing make sense for hoteliers?

— *Low cost*: Email is relatively inexpensive, pennies per email compared to $1 to $3 or more per direct mail.

— *Reach:* Almost instant outreach to an expansive client base, one email blast can be equivalent to thousands of sales calls.

— *Protects brand integrity:* Enables promotion of the latest specials on a one-to-one basis to a pre-selected audience without announcing to the world the latest discounts.

— *Personalisation*: The recipient thinks this is a personalised invitation at a preferred customer rate.

— *Instant gratification*: People are at their computers most of the day and can receive, respond, forward, and print email almost immediately.

— *Rich Media*: Email marketing comes in various styles: text, e-Newsletters, HTML messages like a postcard or survey. The hotel gets its message across with sound, color, animation, video, whatever is most appropriate.

— *Results*: Outcomes based, from knowing who opened the message, clicked on which links, how much time spent viewing each page, completed a transaction, or forwarded the email.

Travel agents that use the Internet and email are exactly the travel agents hoteliers must reach. These agents are likely to visit hotel websites, book online, and even boast hotel web-only promotions in their own marketing efforts to preferred clients. Research from the most respected travel organisations, such as ARC, ASTA, IATA and Plog

Research, as well as leading travel industry trade publications shows that:

— 96 percent of agents send and receive e-mail

— 79 percent of agents receive e-mail travel requests from clients

— 54 percent of agents e-mail clients with special offers or incentives

In the aftermath of September 11th, many New York City hoteliers teamed up to create joint marketing campaigns. Two notable campaigns were the popular "America Loves NY" and "This Week's Top Hotel Deals in NY", produced by Hospitality eBusiness Strategies. These HTML email campaigns ran on a weekly basis over the course of 6 months and provided links back to the hotel websites.

Advantages of Internet

The hospitality industry activities presented on the Internet have many advantages, but one should not underrestimate possible disadvantages this new medium might cause. Many authors are trying to determine advantages and disadvantages from doing business over the Internet. Benefits or competitive advantages of using the Internet in the hospitality industry are:

1) Service improvements concerning:
   - — large choice of access to a WEB site
   - — faster payment processing
   - — reduced delivery time for many products
   - — faster and greater availability of support literature
   - — more detailed and particularised
2) Low costs of:
   - — marketing

— processing of booking and payments
— automation of tasks
— establishing direct links between the producer and the consumer
— distribution

3) Differentiation from competition:
— creating, presenting and selling high-quality, distinctive products

4) Creating up-to-date enterprise image

5) Information usage including the following concepts:
— addressability
— interactivity
— flexibility
— accessibility

6) Efficiency i11 operational management and communication

7) Obtain know-how through discussion with news groups on the Internet

Potential disadvantages or threats of Internet usage in the hospitality industry are:

1) Characteristics of tourism product and services as being fragmented and difficult to evaluate

2) Standardisation of legal procedures of doing business over the Internet

3) The problem of inefficient accessability to the WEB site/unfavourable indexing by search engines

4) Bad quality of individual WEB sites which might damage whole destination image

5) Nonprofessional detennination of purpose the WEB site is supposed to fulfil.

Great competitiveness in the hospitality industry bears enormous challenge for economic development and determines its perfonnance in the global market. The dominant key in achieving success in e-business and consequently competitive position is the quality which can be obtained only by using the Internet as one of the leading instruments of achieving (Total Quality Management), TQM.

Today there is a great amount and many kinds of tourism WEB sites from different tourism sectors, all of which have different purposes and thus providing different kinds of information The fast growth of travel and tourism information on this new medium is caused by customers' demand for higher service levels, better quality of information and tendency to book shorter vacations and to travel more spontaneous.

The WEB is a vast sea of information. The user can access immense amounts of travel-related information, but the sites that provide information about a destination are very badly organised, the information is distrubuted and unstructured. To the traveller seeking for reliable information to plan a trip, the WEB is becoming more and more a time consuming horror where one gets easily lost.

Thus, a good site that serves as a useful tool to plan a trip has to overcome these limitations. Research on tourism WEB sites have started emphasising the importance of creating effective WEB sites. However, research on the effectiveness of tourism WEB sites are not being conducted sufficiently. In addition, most of them were conducted on the basis of content analysis.

An important feature of the Web as a medium is that it is the consumer who is actively searching for information about products or brands in which they are interested. In effect the consumer is "pre-screened" and shows both interest and involvement in visiting the web site. While on the Web, the consumer can also provide instantaneous feedback to the marketer. All the feedback, and indeed, every "click" or "hit" the user makes can be memorised by the web server.

Through the application of the IT data mining technique, companies can find patterns within their internal customer data and make sense of data or turn data into meaningful marketing information. For instance, the visitation record of an online brochure may show the total number of hits, the distribution of the hits among the pages and across time, the order of the pages been accessed.

The user's visitation data can be easily combined with user profile information from user registrations through online visit cards or questionnaires and used to uncover the consumers' interest and the patterns of demand and buying behaviour. This in turn leads to identification of likely target segments, often niches based on specific benefit sought. Armed with such information, organisations can refine their targets and develop specific means to achieve true one - to- one marketing.

The appropriate use of user profile and surfing behaviour data can improve the effectiveness and efficiency of market segmentation and targeting. This is because the traditional approach to market segmentation is often based simplistically on geographical, demographic and economic variables while the psycho, behavioural or lifestyle data is costly to collect and difficult to measure and compare.

In Internet marketing, it is easier to collect these data from potentially each and every user of the company web site, though tangible rewards such as free prize draws and free membership, are often needed to attract users to fill in web forms. It is even a great deal simpler and more effective in market targeting as the email messages and even tailor-made web-pages can reach the intended receiver with little cost. It is possible to set up "virtual" or cyber - communities for each target market niche in the form of news-groups through which consumers with similar interest and behaviour patterns can be sent with relevant product offering and other information from the marketer. Members of such Internet communities can regularly exchange information between them and strengthen a sense of belonging.

One of the major advantages of the Internet in marketing is that the tourist can here be a value creator for tourism companies through redefining the labour division between the marketer and the tourist in providing tourist experiences. This is because, on the one hand, tourists can provide individual preferences for or specifications of holiday packages through feedback in the forms of web forms, email messages or simply the 'clicking' patterns, which the tourism marketer can use to development new products or tailor-make existing products to suit the needs of particular consumer(s). In this sense, the Internet has accelerated a shift in the nature of products from mass produced and tangible to customised and information based.

The role of the Internet in pricing is based on its ability in processing and exchanging large amount of data instantaneously with a great number of people. This information processing capacity enables a company to analyse relevant pricing data effectively and quickly. The information exchange capacity enables firms to set and change prices in real time and also facilitates online bidding and flexible pricing. Both of these qualities of the Net are extremely useful in tourism marketing.

The major tour operators in the UK, for example, produce some 2,000 to 3,000 brochure pages annually, most pages feature a price panel with perhaps 100 separate prices, making a total of about a quarter of a million individual prices. The sheer number of prices, together with the fact that most brochures are launched 10 months in advance of the holiday season, mean that pricing in the travel industry is extremely difficult. Since it is unpractical to set the prices for such a great number of holidays on the bases on demand analysis or competition research, most operators simply follow a cost-plus policy with little regard to the market changes in the months to follow. Even an operator wishes to adjust its holidays prices it is a costly and cumbersome process as new price panels have to be printed and distributed to the travel agencies.

With the help of a web-based reservation system, the task can be a great deal easier. A tour operator can make real-time adjustment to its thousands of holiday prices at a touch of a button in response to competition moves and demand changes. A special late-booking section can also be included in the main web site to promote "left-over" holidays at the last minute to solve the problems of over-supply or under-demand in the package tour industry which has become a chronic issue in the UK during the last decade or so.

In Internet marketing, the potential for price discrimination is diminished given the enhanced capability of consumers to identity the least expensive source, regardless of supplier or location. The skilled consumer could have the "perfect knowledge" of market prices, which could facilitate the realisation, to certain extent, of "perfection competition" at the national and global markets. This will lead to the increasing standardisation of prices across companies or even borders, especially for the undifferentiated products such as airline seats, beach holidays and city breaks. Other applications of pricing on the Web including bidding and flexible pricing - many web-based businesses allow customers to bid for products on their sites.

Customers commit to the sale if the price is agreed upon. The bidding locks in customers to the sale and the committed price. This is a flexible pricing strategy where the buying capacity of the customer reflects in the eventual price. Companies such as Ebay.com and Bid.com have developed a model where other vendors can place products up for bids. Airlines could sell seats on over-demanded flights or routes through online bidding to the highest bidders to generate extra revenue.

Tour operators may use online bidding in a different manner to market special holidays the demand for which may be extremely difficult to estimate in advance. For example, a tour operator can put on its web site the details of a package holiday to the moon and the total cost (including profit margins) for a group, say 50 travellers, the more people bid the lower the price for each traveller. This way of pricing could well enhance the operator's image and profitability, as it is both an innovative marketing and sound financial approach.

The uniqueness of the Internet as a means of distribution is based on the fact that it exists in "cyberspace" thus physical phenomena such as location and distance are less significant or even irrelevant. For the producer, the Web enables it to have direct links with consumers at a low cost therefore provides it with the opportunity of "disintermediation". For the retailer, the Web threatens its livelihood and changes its critical success factor from location, location, location to access, access, access. For the wholesaler, web-based business means it can bypass retailers while at the same time risk being bypassed by the producers.

The foremost role of the Web in tourism distribution is the direct electronic reservation and transactions between tourism product supplier and consumers. Aldridge et al argues that direct marketing is the name of the game on the Internet, offering both consumers and marketers greater control and lower potential costs of access due to the conveniences of the Net.

Because direct channels may be producer-direct or intermediary-direct, the potential for channel conflict will be magnified. In order to assuage channel conflict and price competition between direct-sellers and retailers, both producers and intermediaries will have to develop augmented product features and unique benefits. For example, direct online booking of airline tickets often carries special benefits not available from travel agents, such as extra frequent-flyer miles; while purchasing an airline ticket from an online travel agency may also benefit from such services as hotel reservations and travel insurance.

Wireless Services in Hospitality Industry

Hospitality companies have a unique opportunity to increase the value of their core products and services by providing a wireless infrastructure for customers to connect to the Internet, check e-mail and utilise corporate applications. In addition, there is a significant opportunity for businesses to benefit from the network by offering customised guest amenities and equipping employees with wireless devices to improve upon current operational inefficiencies.

As the first large retail chain to deploy wireless, Starbucks has established approximately 2,000 wireless-enabled stores worldwide. While there has been an abundance of positive publicity around the deployment, users accessing the network are few and far between. At each location, between one and five people are estimated to be using the service every month, at a rate of $6.00 per hour for one-time use or $39.99 per month for unlimited access. In a similar manner, McDonald's has recently begun a pilot deployment at 10 stores in New York city, with several hundred more planned by year end. Customers receive 60 minutes of wireless access free with the purchase of an Extra Value Meal or can buy access for $3. The deployments are too recent to confirm the degree of success, but the initial pattern seems to be similar to that of Starbucks with relatively low customer usage.

Wireless at McDonald's is a tougher sell because of the typical clientele. With more of a family-oriented environment than other merchants, McDonald's is generally not considered a place where typical customers would bring their laptops. With the model still in its infancy and almost certain to change, businesses must be creative to lure customers into using the infrastructure. One way to do this may include renovation of current facilities to cater to laptop-savvy customers by adding comfortable seats, wireless printers and a workspace with enough room for both a PC and a burger. Another option is to offer free telephone calls via voice-over IP (VOIP), a technology that sends voice over the network in a similar manner as data. While VOIP is currently in development, the functionality will offer significant opportunity for stores of the future.

Above and beyond providing customer access, wireless can offer customised customer experiences and improve upon current operational inefficiencies.In instances where speed of delivery makes or breaks a business, as is the case of McDonald's, creative 'line-buster' solutions can be deployed. These wireless tools range from remote ordering kiosks (staffed or unstaffed) and digital menu boards to devices that automatically control equipment.

Another area where wireless infrastructure is key is within the lodging space. Guest Internet access is becoming a standard amenity throughout the industry and travellers will soon find it as necessary as ice machines and cable television. Industry research recently conducted by IBM indicates the percentage of guests accessing wireless has been seen to exceed 20 percent in some cases, much greater than the uptake at food and beverage outlets. This is a key indicator that wireless is on the rise.

With a significant majority of hotels indicating Internet access can have an impact on occupancy, installing wireless needs to be considered in addition to wired solutions because of greater flexibility, faster implementation, fewer connectivity issues and reduced capital investment. In more and more cases, the availability of in-room, public space and meeting room access is a make-or-break decision for both the independent traveller and meeting planners of small and large group events.

Operational improvements can be realised when wireless devices are used for business functions such as check-in, check-out, bill printing, directions, concierge services, amenity requests, housekeeping, maintenance, point of sale, sales and catering and table management. While the number of these applications currently in use is minimal, redesigning today's core processes tied to wired solutions will allow hotels to operate more efficiently, empower the guests with more resources and respond to customer requests in a more prompt and accurate manner.

Wireless uses a family of specifications known as 802.11 to send high frequency signals to and from enabled devices. The most common standard today, 802.11b, provides acceptable connectivity speeds over a broad range of about 300 feet. Using a different approach, recently deployed 802.11a allows for faster data transmissions, but results in a relatively shorter range. In an attempt to improve upon both the connectivity speeds and range of 802.11a/b, 802.11g is currently in development.

Businesses implement wireless networks for customers and corporate applications two primary ways.

In the first option, a local technology department installs access points as an extension of the wired solution. This allows the business to not only receive all revenue from the network but also tags it with the higher risk. The other option is to lease bandwidth from external providers such as telecom companies (T-Mobile, Sprint) or Cometa Networks, a joint venture of Intel, IBM and AT&T. In this revenue-sharing model, the provider ensures proper security, billing, bandwidth control, network maintenance and technical support.

Using a different approach than installing hotspots, the wireless Internet can also be found through a high-speed cellular system known as 2.5/3G. As an extension to the phone system, wireless devices are given an actual cellular phone number. While the technology is not widespread today and still under development, the portability and flexibility that is opened to users make it a technology that needs to be watched.

Future Trends

In some industries, profits are made on spare parts and maintenance rather than on mainstream products. In the new economy, we may see this business model replicated in the hospitality industry. And for those companies that discount or give away products such as hotel rooms in order to sell linked services, they surely will be redefining the meaning of hospitality. They will also be marketing an array of hospitality and leisure products and services to a customer base that is no longer satisfied with the traditional ways of making such purchases.

Hospitality businesses that traditionally provided room, board, management and marketing may need to rethink their roles in the new economy, particularly as services become more valuable than products. With the rapid growth of "infomediaries" and their facilitation of transactions, hospitality businesses may need to redefine themselves in order to prosper in an increasingly electronic world where one-to-one customisation is the order of the day. But for those contemplating repositioning their companies in an e-business environment, it will be necessary to focus on the current value proposition of the business and determine how it might be reformatted or enhanced to ensure success in the new setting.

But just how prepared is the global hospitality industry to capitalise on some of the opportunities afforded by the emerging new economy? In Arthur Andersen's recently published global survey of technology, Hospitality 2000: The Technology, we addressed some of the issues that the industry is facing. These included the closed nature of our technology architectures, the way in which we collect information on our customers, our investments in Internet, intranet and extranet technologies, and our adoption of electronic commerce.

The results are not especially encouraging and suggest an industry still relatively slow to adapt to e-business. Only 39% of the industry's Web sites, for example, can handle reservations on a real-time basis, and even fewer still (19%), collect customer information. At the same time, just 22% are using "push" marketing programmes and a distinct minority (just 19%), have extranets to suppliers or customers. But these adoption rates are nonetheless projected to grow and we should, therefore, expect our industry's leaders to be far more attuned to the needs of an e-business environment in the years to come.

As information technology (IT) is used to facilitate a company's entry into the world of electronic commerce, our industry's leadership will also need to overcome a natural tendency to be disappointed by the role of IT in achieving competitive advantage. For many years IT was seen as a mechanism to support back office finance and accounting functions. In the future, it inevitably will be one of the principal drivers of value creation in the new economy. But we should not be mislead by IT—in e-business, it will be the strategy, not the technology that will make the difference between success and failure. But having the strategy in place is only the first step. It must be linked to every part of the business.

Cost of E-business

With the costs of playing in the e-business world escalating rapidly, hospitality executives should consider the four phases of what might be called the "E-Business Lifecycle." The first of these—E-Business Strategy Development and Planning—must address the market and competitive context, articulate the vision and opportunity, outline the strategy and the business case, and identify the risks. In recent years, we have frequently seen hospitality businesses put up a Web site on the Internet and consider this an e-business strategy. But without a strategy for this new form of commerce and the business planning process to drive it, such reactionary approaches stand little chance for success.

Once the plan is in place, an e-business design phase can commence to address site design, lay out the business architecture, identify the technical infrastructure, plan for performance, availability and capacity, and deal with tax issues and enterprise security. Following the design phase, E-Business implementation will prepare for the launch with training and change enablement, implementation and integration, testing and roll-out. Once in place, E-Business Operations will need to be supported by IT and audit services, Web site activity analysis and Web site maintenance. Finally, measurement systems will need to be established to monitor performance.

As industry executives embark on this e-business lifecycle, they will need in the first stage to clearly establish the business case for investing in new technologies, systems and organisations by addressing both the cost reduction and revenue enhancement benefits. On the revenue side, there are a number of factors to consider. These include the company's ability to identify and recruit the most valuable customers; the ability to seamlessly cross-sell the company's products and services, as well as those of alliance partners; the ability to retain valuable customers and reduce attrition (especially relevant in a world of questionable brand loyalty); and finally, when and how to eliminate costly and unnecessary discounts through revenue optimisation.

In this kind of environment, the property management system will no longer hold sway as the center of the hospitality universe, but will become just one in a series of customer touch-points that will increasingly include the Internet. These touch-points will ultimately need to be fully integrated into a customer information system supported by sophisticated data warehousing and data mining technologies.

Adding to the industry's costs in this portrait of the future is the cost of grafting e-business technologies onto the industry's legacy systems. At a certain stage, it may make sense to start from scratch and ensure that every system is Web-enabled. This would allow a total interface for a high-growth e-business, thereby maximising the customer relationship management opportunities that it presents.

As to the role of the Internet, its comprehensive reach and ubiquitous nature has already ensured its central place in the new economy. But how should we evaluate whether an Internet application is deserving of our attention? Firstly, productivity on the Internet in the years to come will be vastly improved by much higher bandwidth than is currently in place. And with higher bandwidth will come applications that can benefit from such extra capacity delivering tightly focused and reliable content to an increasingly sophisticated and demanding e-customer. If an Internet application is to succeed in the future, it will therefore need to be designed to capitalise on this coming reality.

Secondly, an Internet application needs to form a community of some sort because without a sense of place, albeit of the virtual sort participants will not have that all-important sense of belonging. And as with the industrial revolution, which drew a disparate population to centers of economic activity, so will such "intranet communities" grow in value as their populations increase in size and their economic product expands. For larger businesses that form such communities, they are developing new revenue sources and are reinventing their relationships with customers, employees, suppliers and partners. Smaller companies intent on participating in this new environment, may need to be content as a participant in an established community, rather than trying to take on the creation of a community itself. It is better, perhaps, to be one of many players in a successful space than struggling to establish an identity in a world surrounded by also-rans.

Whether large or small, community developers and marketers of the virtual sort will have to recognise that what may have appeared cool in the physical world to generations brought up in the old economy will not work in the world of e-business. Being cool and staying that way in order to get and keep attention will remain a constant challenge, especially for those keen to nurture a younger generation of travelers brought up on MTV and the Web.

Finally, the successful Internet application needs to improve service while reducing transaction costs, particularly as the balance of power in the buy/sell relationship continues its inexorable migration from sellers to buyers. Service improvement strategies will be nothing new for hospitality businesses, but it is noteworthy that service (rather than on-time delivery, price or other concerns) is the top factor that encourages return e-business. This must be an area of focus since the current growth of e-business appears destined to outpace the supporting infrastructure and its related service at least over the short term. But as hospitality executives know, delivering good service can be expensive.

Scaling the types of service response to the circumstances is a growing need, but one that can be modulated if the value of each customer can be distinguished and the response adjusted accordingly. In considering the opportunities in hospitality e-business, industry leaders should take stock of the dynamics that are occurring in the new economy and plan accordingly. It is probably easy to dismiss the e-business world as a playground for others with products and services that are more obviously applicable. But our industry is changing, as is the world around us.

Brand Strategies & Marketing

Hotel owners and independent managers play an important role in deciding on the brand strategy to be pursued by individual properties. To some, the production of a branded reservation system and the impact on average room rate are the acid tests of what works and what doesn't. Other attributes of a brand are perhaps just as relevant - consistency, sales office support, the matching of the brand's positioning with the property's optimum segment mix, image, future development plans on a system-wide basis and the impact of additional brand development in the local marketplace are some of the other factors to be considered. Understanding the total dynamic at work in selecting the optimum brand is a complex task that thus requires careful analysis.

A marketing plan, like any business plan, must address three components - strategy, organisation and capital. Strategy outlines the vision for the future; organisation addresses the people requirements, the skills and the processes; and finally capital deals with how financial resources can be deployed and what return they can expect.

In brand marketing, these areas are especially relevant in view of the large amounts of capital that tend to be deployed in the constant search for the customer and in the efforts to develop and retain customer loyalty. As hotel owners and operators consider the competitive dynamics of tomorrow's marketspace, they will need to plan fully if their brand strategies are to deliver on the promise of customer access and loyalty.

Product consistency, as a result, remains one of the most critical issues in the hotel industry. For new brands that were launched in the 1980s and have reached critical mass, there appears to be little difficulty in establishing product consistency, especially when most of the product is new construction and involves smaller, more simply engineered properties.

Other brands that rely on converting older facilities have frequently had difficulties, typically when they are under pressure to build up a chain quickly to reach critical mass. Balancing the demands for growth in a global brand-oriented marketplace with the desire for product integrity and consistency will always be a tough challenge. The outlook for those companies still struggling with product inconsistency remains somewhat cloudy.

A salvation for such companies in the past has been a strong development environment in which there is plenty of new construction. Since another development cycle is unlikely to be financed in the near future, inconsistent brand portfolios will become the repository for those properties that cannot afford to pay for higher-valued brands that in turn demand adherence to a core mission satisfying and exceeding customer expectations concerning the product they buy.

Given these complex factors, we again pose the question Is brand marketing in the hospitality industry more an art than a science? There is little question that brand marketing has been lacking in " science" historically. With little understanding of the customer - the who, the how, the what and the where - many brands were established purely as growth vehicles for companies that relied on other people's capital to expand.

As capital becomes more discerning in the future and as the customer becomes the primary focus of attention, this will inevitably change. Technology's impact will also force and support the move towards making brand marketing the science that it must become to support the successful hotel organisations of the next century.

Mass Customisation

Mass customisation is neither a simple strategy to undertake organisationally and operationally, nor is it a simple concept to comprehend. Hart defined mass customisation by using two distinct definitions:

— *The visionary definition*: The ability to provide customers with anything they want profitably, any time they want it, anywhere they want it, any way they want it.

— *The practical definition*: The use of flexible processes and organisational structures to produce varied and often individually customised products and services at the low cost of a standardised, mass production system.

According to Hart, the goal in the first definition will rarely be achieved by an organisation. It was considered a transcendent, absolute idea that exists solely as an ideal. The goal in the second definition is not the "anything-at-any-time" promised by the visionary definition.

It is "to ascertain, from the customer's perspective, the range within which a given product or service can be meaningfully customised (i.e. differentiated) for that customer, and then to facilitate the customer's choice of options from within that range." He lamented that the concept of producing tailor-made or partially tailor-made goods or services according to customer desire, with very short cycle times and mass production efficiencies, is a more realizable goal than that offered by the visionary definition.

In essence, mass customisation is a hybrid technique by which a company churns out products in typical assembly-line fashion yet can add unique features to individual orders. This requires a flexible manufacturing system that anticipates a wide range of options.

However, due to the vast differences in customer preferences, mass customisation, too, can produce unnecessary cost and complexity. Therefore, it is crucial that managers must examine thoroughly what kind of customisation their customers would value before they adopt this new strategy.

Hart further identified four key decision factors:

1. *Customer sensitivity*. The first question companies need to ask themselves is: Do your customers care whether you offer more customisation? If the answer is no, the mass customisation potential is limited.
2. *Process amenability*. This is a multifaceted area. The first obvious question is: Does your process technology, which exists in your area allow you to customise your

product or service to individual customers? If it does, the next question is how extensive an overhaul is required to incorporate this technology into your existing process and how much investment will be required?

Another part of process amenability is marketing. Since the goal of mass customisation is products or services tailored to individual customers, an important question for companies to ask is: Does the marketing department have access to the level of detail regarding customer needs and the capacity to analyse such information? A third consideration is design. Is your company capable of translating custom needs into actual specifications? The last consideration under this factor is production and distribution. Partly depending on the form and nature of product or service, the flexibility of the production system to handle mass customisation is a critical point here.

3. *Competitive environment.* The major question here is: Are there competitive forces that would enhance or detract from the advantage your company would gain from implementing mass customisation? In other words, would you be the first in your market with a mass-customised product? How long would it take for competitors to react? And how will your competitors' customers react?

4. *Organisational readiness.* The last decision factor requires an honest assessment of your company's culture and resources. Is your company able and ready to capitalise on the opportunity inherent in mass customisation? Organisational change requires enlightened leadership, open-minded management, and financial resources. Hence, mass customisation strategy is unique to the company developing and implementing it. There is no "cookie-cutter" approach to creating such a strategy. Mass customisation

strategy that works for one company might not work for another company.

In 1997, Gilmore and Pine identified four distinct approaches to customisation, which are collaborative, adaptive, cosmetic, and transparent. They advocated that when designing or redesigning a product, process, or business unit, managers should choose an approach or a mix of some or all of the four approaches to serve their own particular set of customers.

1. *Collaborative customisation*. This approach follows three steps: first to conduct a dialogue with individual customers to help them articulate their needs; second, to identify the precise offering that fulfills those needs; and third, to make customised products for them. Collaborative customisation is most appropriate for businesses whose customers cannot easily articulate what they want and grow frustrated when forced to select from a plethora of options.
2. *Adaptive customisation*. Adaptive customisers offer one standard, but customisable, product that is designed so that users can alter it themselves. This approach is appropriate for businesses whose customers want the product to perform in different ways on different occasions, and available technology makes it possible for them to customise the product easily on their own.
3. *Cosmetic customisation*. This approach is appropriate when customers use a product the same way and differ only in how they want it presented. in other words, the standard offering is packaged specially for each customer.
4. *Transparent customisation*. This approach is appropriate when customers' needs are predictable or can easily be deduced, and especially when customers do not want to state their needs repeatedly. Offerings were customised within a standard package for individual customers.

To sum up, collaborative customisers change the product itself in addition to changing some aspect of the presentation while a cosmetic customiser changes only the presentation of the product. A transparent customiser uses a standard representation to mask the customisation of the product and finally adaptive customisers change neither the product nor the representation of the product but they provide the customer with the ability to change both the product's function and/or its presentation to meet their needs.

Hospitality industry has generally preferred to keep wages low, thus avoiding the need for technological innovation, particularly in the actual delivery of its services. Although technology has been used extensively in a supporting role to enhance performance and effectiveness, (e.g., computer reservation system, air control technology, accounting system) there has been a great reluctance to replace human service providers with technologically driven alternatives. However, in recent years, some "tinkering" of mass customisation has occurred in selected areas in the lodging industry.

Industries, which are less dependent on the human interactions have adopted laborsaving technology. As a result, these industries have been able to improve wage levels and enhance career opportunities for employees while keeping costs under control. For example, banks replace human tellers with automatic teller machines, which not only save labor costs but also offer 24-hour service year round. This kind of convenience provided to their customers can be considered a great customisation.

New Opportunities for Hospitality

Assisted living represents a prime opportunity for hospitality companies willing to use the core competencies of hospitality to develop and operate communities for seniors. While most of the major hospitality entities have merged, consolidated or entered new market segments in last few years. only one hospitality company is currently a major player in the assisted living industry, Marriott International, which expanded into assisted living in 1989, now occupies the number two position on the chart for the top 25 U.S. Senior housing Owners and is ranked third in the top 25 U.S. Senior Housing Managers. In June of 1996, Marriott completed its merger with Forum Group, in the process acquiring an additional 42 assisted living facilities. As of October 1997, Marriott operated 82 assisted living communities, and the company plans to triple that number in the next five years.

Does Marriott's path in assisted living make sense for other hospitality companies? Clearly there are "cross-over" resources and skills between the hospitality and assisted living industries. Food and beverage and other processes in hospitality can be translated into assisted living operations. Indeed, hospitality companies with brands that represent service and quality have two of the most import ant ingredients when consumers make buying decisions in this industry. There are also challenges for a hospitality company expanding in this industry, however, given its mission of providing care services to the elderly. Nevertheless, the prospects may be attractive to hospitality companies with significant resources, given that assisted living is likely to be the fastest-growing segment in the long-term care industry.

Three primary demographic trends will shape growth of the assisted living industry in the next few decades. Advances in nutrition and medical science have resulted in an increased life expectancy, and consequently growing numbers of elderly people. Many seniors are living longer, more active lives.

Second, as an increasing number of women enter the workforce, their ability to serve as the primary caregiver to aging parents has been greatly reduced, thus changing the role of the family in providing elderly care. Third, a greater number of elderly are now living in isolation in many countries.

In the United States, for example, the average family moves once every five years. Many families are widely scattered, leaving elderly parents alone. Family structures have radically changed in recent decades. The end result is an elderly population that has been left without the traditional sources of assistance needed to perform their daily activities. Families must increasingly rely on alternative solutions to fulfill their previous roles as caregivers.

Proactive companies in the assisted living industry have stepped in to provide these services to a market that is forecast to grow at a record pace. The number of people aged 65 and over in the United States is currently 34 million, accounting for 13 percent of the total population. That number is projected to grow to 69 million, or 20 percent of the total population, by the year 2030. The number of elderly will only increase with the aging of the baby boom generation, those individuals born between 1946 and 1964. As this generation ages and retires, an increasing number of people over the age of 75 will require some level of care or assistance during the final years of their lives. The number of people aged 85 and over is currently 3.7 million and is projected to increase to 8.5 million by the year 2030. Demand will be driven by increases in how long people live. The average life expectancy for women aged 65 is projected to increase from 84.2 years in 1995 to 87.4 years in the year 2050.

The demographic shift in the European Union (EU) may be even more extreme than in North America, where the demographic structure of society is more greatly influenced by immigration and slightly higher birth rates. The population aged 60 or over in the European Union had climbed by 50 percent in recent years, reaching 68.6 million by 1992. Estimates place the number of older people in the European Union at 80 to 100 million by the year 2020, of which 27 to 29 million are estimated to be over 80 years old. The average life expectancy in Europe is estimated at 78 years for men and 82.5 years for women. This is reported slightly lower in the United Kingdom at 77.6 years for men and 81.7 years for women.

Also of urgent concern is the financial strength of the aging in the European Union, with poverty remaining a source of worry for many older people in EU countries. A 1993 Eurostate survey revealed that 48 percent of older people in the then 12 EU countries had financial difficulties. Health and social services or older people vary widely across Europe. Generally, however, the trend is toward de-emphasising institutionalisation and promoting private care or assistance. Although needs and resources vary greatly among the elderly in North America and Europe, assisted living will almost certainly sustain significant growth in the near future for a variety of reasons:

— Increased life expectancy of population as a whole, and of the assisted living target market;
— Decreased need for acute care by elderly;
— Increased relative wealth of elderly population;
— Decreased role of traditional substitutes to assisted living, particularly hospitals and nursing homes, as a result of cost pressures;
— Increased awareness and acceptance of assisted living services as an alternative to family care;
— Decreased lime available to traditional care providers, principally family members, creating the need for alternatives.

Inspired by the Dutch and Scandinavian systems, assisted living programmes originally offered housing and sheltered services for the frail elderly. Today, the industry provides long-term care in a homelike environment at less expensive rates than nursing homes. Elderly residents gain an ability to live a more autonomous lifestyle, while enjoying the comfort and security of on-site services, including health programmes and other types of support. As residents age, their level of need increases, and the community becomes responsible for providing more complex levels of care. This is commonly referred to as "aging in place." Residents are able to customise their level of care based upon their needs.

A Merrill Lynch industry report indicates that the average assisted living community comprises 58 separate private living units. A typical resident is a widowed or single female, 84 years of age, who needs assistance with three activities of daily living. Some 30 to 40 percent of residents suffer from Alzheimer's or some other form of dementia.

Due to the focus on lower acuity care, assisted living communities can offer the elderly the level of care that is individually required at prices that are typically two-thirds of what a nursing home would charge. Most assisted living communities in the United States offer a tiered pricing schedule in which residents pay a basic rate for room and board, and are then charged additional fees depending on the level of service they select.

This economic structure is beneficial for both the provider and the customer. The customer is able to obtain an individualised level of service at prices substantially less than at other higher acuity centers, like nursing homes. The provider is able to continuously serve customers as their needs change.

Assisted living companies in the United States are currently able to offer affordable services to their residents with monthly costs for assisted living (housing, meals and additional services) ranging from $1,500 - $3,000,9 with certain markets ranging as high as $6,000 - $7,000. Private payers represent 96 percent of the industry's total revenue. Costs to residents could increase substantially, however, depending on the extent of future regulation.

While U.S. nursing homes and other healthcare providers are heavily regulated on a federal level currently, the American assisted living industry is free of many of the costly compliance burdens of federal regulation. Regulation of the assisted living industry, however, looms on the horizon as the expansion of this industry has stimulated greater scrutiny of assisted living providers.

The assisted living industry is highly fragmented, with a growing trend toward consolidation. The supply of communities has been unable to keep pace with demand and consolidations have begun to accelerate. The top 50 operators in the industry housed an estimated 20 percent of the residents in 1996 until their needs required that they move to nursing homes or other higher acuity programmes. Providers look to gain critical mass and strengthen their presence in particular geographic regions. This environment will create opportunities for strong operators and developers with loyal employees, an established marketing process, and access to capital.

7

New Realities of Hospitality Sales

The basics of hotel sales have changed forever. The sheer size of most markets and technology dictate that sales becomes more efficient and effective. While the skill sets of selling techniques haven't changed, the way we locate and develop new business has to change. Gone are the days when a sales person could walk the street and cold call everyone within a three or five-mile radius. Gone are the days when a cold phone call was returned and all it required was persistence.

Even "backyard marketing" requires new approaches. The sheer size of the "backyards" of most urban and suburban sub-markets is too large for almost any hotel to physically or cold call on the telephone every potential business. Another dilemma is the "list." Many sales people are given lists of prospects in their market, trade show attendees from very large venues, etc.

The "dead files" are another prospect source resorted to out of desperation. If these were such good leads, why aren't they in the active trace system to begin with? Sales departments are pulling out boxes or going through old filing cabinets of files that haven't been worked or followed up upon in years. Unfortunately, in many sales departments the task of calling the dead files often falls to the newest member of the team or worse, the sales assistant. These people are usually inadequately trained and, in the best-case scenario, given a list of questions to ask and told to follow up with a packet of sales information. If any of these lead sources sounds familiar, read on - there is a better way of dealing with each of these. But it is not the old "basics," it is a new way slicing the lists and looking at the prospecting process.

Sales is not a job where you can just show up in the morning. Sales people need to listen to the news, read the business sections of the newspaper — pay attention to what's going on in the business world surrounding them. The good ones do — the ones that don't won't be around long! Pay attention to the stock market. Those industry sectors whose stocks are rising have the money to conduct meetings and pay your rates. Once you know which industries are performing well, do a search for those in your market.

If a "dead" file hasn't given you business in two years or more, treat it as a new prospect for qualifying purposes. Before you call, check to see which industry sector it is in. In prioritising the trace files, give first consideration to those that are doing well. This applies to associations serving the profitable industries sectors. In this economy there are losers that are losing big but there are winners who are quietly making money out there.

Smart prospecting takes more time, but is more profitable in the amount of time expended. Call activity becomes more productive and "sales burn out" is less likely. Next month we will deal with effective ways to approach new business prospects, calling and leaving messages just doesn't cut it any more! In this economy, and make no mistake, the recovery is likely to be delayed until 2004 at the earliest and even then will not return to the robust times of the mid-nineties.

Role of Internet in Hotel Sales

Hotel bookings through the Internet, whether on franchise web sites or electronic distribution channels, have risen exponentially. This has led many hotels and hotel companies to re-allocate sales and marketing resources to managing and manipulating their positioning on the Internet. They are quite correct in doing so — this is a trend that is not only not going away but will continue this kind of growth for at least a few years into the future.

This percentage increase, unfortunately, has not been characteristic of most hotel sales departments and, as a result, the precious marketing resources available to them have, in many cases, been reduced to accommodate the expenditures on Internet channels and web presence. As a result, many hotel sales people have become frustrated and discouraged to the point that they wonder if there is a continuing role for them as this trend continues.

The traditional methods and modes of conducting hotel sales will not produce the results that will alleviate this concern. It is a simple case of "if you keep on doing what you have always done, you will continue to get what you have always gotten." In today's environment, that leads to diminishing returns as travel and meeting planners turn to the Internet more and more to evaluate rate and amenity positioning prior to ever contacting a hotel. Often, the second step is to visit the web site of a particular property, again prior to contacting the sales department.

Hotels need to include the sales departments in their Internet positioning and web design so that the message and offering is consistent across the customer touch points. In addition, sales departments need to embrace the technology and use the Internet to become more productive and efficient in conducting hotel sales at every step of the sales process. For example:

Target Market Prospecting: In an attempt to locate new markets as existing ones are producing less, the decision is often made to target markets that previously were ignored. This can range from government (all of a sudden per diems don't look so bad from a rate standpoint), SMERF, Affinity groups, etc.

Traditional Sales: Locate existing or dead files for prospects in these target markets then begin contacting them one at a time. If they weren't producing before, why would they now and how long will it take you to contact enough prospects in a new market to ascertain its depth?

Cyber Sales: Conduct a web search that becomes increasingly specific until a prospect list or database can be located on related web sites.

Market Penetration Strategy: In most cases, it is impossible to ascertain the depth of a market or begin to penetrate it without making contact with a significant number of prospects. How to do this efficiently?

Traditional Sales: They are still contacting the "dead" files. Contacting one individual or organisation with a phone call is very time consuming and not very efficient.

Cyber Sales: Develops an email postcard or an email message with a benefits tease, copies and pastes email addresses into a group on the email address book, puts each name on the email as a bcc. and sends it off to groups of ten or twenty at a time to avoid the appearance of "spamming" with the ISP.

Initial Approach: The name of a prospective organisation and key contact information is available. Now what?

Traditional Sales: Pick up the telephone and call them. Upon routing to their voice mail, leave a message with your name, the hotel's name and phone number. Trace it for two weeks, repeat process.

Cyber Sales: Locate the e-mail address on the web site or call the central number, press zero (normally there is still a human available) and ask for the contact's email address. A recent client was absolutely amazed at how willing the receptionist was to give out the email address.

This is only a brief glimpse at how hotel sales departments can incorporate the Internet into their every day activities to contact more prospects more efficiently. Each of the examples above are just the beginning of the techniques that hotel sales departments can use to incorporate the internet into their activities to penetrate target markets, develop new prospects and maintain relationships.

People are now used to initiating and building business relationships through email, instant messaging, etc. Once we have "touched" them enough times electronically, it is then possible to make a telephone appointment to build on the relationship. A telephone appointment is more efficient than leaving voice mails. The message here is that hotel sales departments can use the Internet in many ways to become more productive and efficient.

Generation of Revenue

One of the new realities of hotel sales is accountability. If sales people are not prepared to operate in that environment then it is time for them to find a new career path. If sales people are just waiting for the boom times to return when they weren't held accountable, move on, the "boom" times are not coming back any time soon.

Focus is not about getting organised — it is about being prioritised. The organisation of bits of paper is not focus. The organisation of files or the folders in your Inbox are not focus. Focus is about deciding which things are priorities that generate new revenue and maintain business. There are things that sales people and their managers can do to assist in developing a "focused" orientation:

Analyse Daily Activity: Force yourself to write down everything you do for a day and for how long. No cheating! Review it with management.

Prioritise Activity: Calling existing clients to have a chat is not a priority — there is enough time at the end of the day to leave a message, send an email and say "hello." Messages and emails are wonderful things — they don't take long to write and they let the other person know you are thinking about them. Priorities are contracts, proposals, site inspections, finding new prospects — everything associated with revenue generation.

Reduce or Eliminate Interruptions: Close the door; post a sign indicating that you are doing sales activity and that unless it is an emergency, please leave a note. You will be amazed at how few notes are left.

Prioritise the Task List: This assumes that most of you are using or have access to a contact management programme. It could be ACT!, Outlook or any of the good hotel-specific programmes on the market. They work only if you use them. You have the capability in many of these to assign a priority to each activity. Assign the highest priority to those that impact revenue generation. The rest can wait.

The fact of the matter is that it is hard selling anything these days given the restrictions that apply to sales activities. Someone forgot to tell the bureaucrats who endorsed the no-call lists, the restrictions on unsolicited faxes and the current proposals to deal with spam that nothing in this country happens until a sale is made. That's free enterprise, a free market economy.

These techniques must work or no one would be using them. It is very difficult to be a sales person of any kind these days. The noble profession of sales has been given a black eye and this rubs off on our hotel sales people. While the limitations on telephone calls are not restricted in a Business-to-Business environment, the generally negative attitude toward sales people has permeated our target clients' mindsets as well. They don't answer their phone; they allow it to go to voice mail. Hence, why "dialing for dollars" no longer works in most markets. Try cold calling in a large office building in most major markets today — security will be on your tail in five minutes, if it takes them that long!

An article by Alan Webber, a founding editor of Fast Company, appeared in USA Today on November 3, 2002 entitled Companies Repeat Mistake of Cutting Investment in Workers. "One of the easiest ways to make your numbers look better is to cut back on 'non-essential' items. Training and Development can be axed. ...(This includes) programmes that give executives — or any workers — new ideas, new techniques, new tactics and new approaches to winning in the workplace. Once the tyranny of numbers sets in, almost any investment in people is an easy target."

Alan Webber goes on to remind us that in the 1970's American industry was preoccupied with the "numbers" or as he puts it, financial engineering. The Japanese weren't — they invested in their people and subsequently outperformed their US competitors in terms of quality and price.

The world of sales is changing rapidly and will continue to do so. It is tougher and requires a paradigm shift in the way we conduct hotel sales. It is an exciting change for those who embrace it. A hotel sales person asked the following question after a presentation to her company's annual meeting. "With the role of technology so prevalent in our industry will we still need sales people?"

What we need to do is re-define the relationships between sales and operations, especially revenue management, sales and marketing, sales and reservations. It's not just the sales staff that needs to rethink how they are going to solicit and how to use the new tech tools, it is the entire revenue generating engine of the hotel that needs to make a paradigm shift in how we do business effectively in relation to how our current and target clients have changed.

Managing the Sales Process

Five years ago, when demand was high and the sales function was relegated to answering the phone and taking the order, it was relatively easy for General Managers to keep an eye on things in the sales department. Unemployment was at historic lows and in order to keep positions filled, we were reluctant to expect too much or discipline an under performing employee. There was a tendency to keep the chair warm rather than let a position go unfilled.

Times have changed both in terms of demand of demand and the employment pool but often the attitudes of management have not. Sales people represent a distinct management challenge. The good ones are bright, aggressive, able to sell their managers as well as their clients but they are also very human.

They like most other employees will take the path of least resistance, need to have expectations made clear and have objective standards of performance by which they are evaluated. Sales people (like everyone else) do not perceive the importance of job duties that are not monitored by their supervisors. If an employee, sales or not, is going to take home the same paycheck whether or not they achieve their goals, why would they do more that the minimum requirements?

GMs have a particular challenge in that they work long hours and very closely with their sales staffs, especially the DOS. It is difficult to maintain an objective and professional distance that allows for the kind of management that gets results. We all have a human need to be liked — leadership is about respect. There are a few simple steps you can take to make your monitoring of the sales effort more effective. They may also make the sales effort more effective.

Refrain from Cronyism – Simply put, this means do not get too close to your DOS or any member of the sales department. (You wouldn't compromise your ability to lead the other department heads by too much socialising – or would you?) It is difficult with a DOS who has worked for you for a long time. It is also difficult with the long hours required working in close quarters in this industry. There has to be a line of familiarity that you don't cross. It negates your ability to lead and manage effectively. You know when you have crossed the line. The GM had worked with this DOS for several years, they played golf once a week and he frequently had the DOS and spouse for dinner at his house. It totally blinded him to the persons deficiencies in job performance and the DOS took complete advantage of the situation.

Have regular sales meetings with a fixed agenda. It should occur at least once a month, preferably once a week at a time when it does not interfere with Prime Selling Hours. (You do know what those are, don't you?) This provides a structured environment in which you can ask the 'tough' questions without sounding picky and irrational. To a sales person, if you just casually ask a question about an account or ask for numbers, they are likely to feel that you are just in a bad mood and it will pass.

In a more structured environment, you can ask specific questions about accounts mentioned on reports, question the content of numbers on the PACE report, etc.. There is an old story, perhaps apocryphal, that Kurt Carlson, the founder of Carlson Companies, used to ask his Division Heads to bring their financials on overheads. He would project pages on a screen and point tone specific number line item on the page. He would then ask what was in this cumulative number. He figured if a Division Head could specifically outline what this represented, they knew and could do the same on any line item in the reports.

Take a course in sales. If you come from another discipline in the industry, learn about basic sales. Read a book, take a course – take a course in sales not related to the industry. There are many fine resources for hotel sales available especially now when that function has become so challenging.

Set realistic goals and involve them in the process. Goal setting should be an objective process. When you let them know what they need to produce and why, then involve them in figuring out how they are going to get there, they understand and ideally buy into the plan. If they don't buy in they will begin to flat their resume. We all have choices – if they feel it is unattainable, they can exercise their choice to walk. If they are really good sales people who feel that unrealistic goals have been foisted upon them, they will do exactly that. You need to let them know that if you feel the goals set by the corporate office are unattainable, you will go to bat for realistic goals given the market circumstance. You have been around the block enough times to know the difference between a challenge and the unattainable.

Be supportive but expect results! If your sales staff is making a ton of calls but producing few results, it could be a skills problem. Offer them some training. When a reasonable amount of time and training effort has passed, don't be afraid to make the tough decision. The fact of the matter is they are uncomfortable at their non-performance and may be happier and more satisfied in another position.

New Hotel Sales Environment

Any farmer can tell you that the most frustrating thing about farming is the lack of control over the environment needed to produce a crop. Drought (such as we have now in the hotel sales environment) means that fewer crops grow and those seeds that do come up produce plants of inferior quality (read lower yield). The crop is diminished and revenue from "farming" declines. Pestilence (we could call this competition) disseminates the crop and makes less of the crop available for harvest (everyone is going after the same business). The "farmer" is dependent on the environment to generate revenue.

Hunters have a different perspective. Hunters go out and actively seek their revenue. If one type of "prey" (market segment) is in short supply, they shift gears and pursue another. Hunters are opportunistic - they have control over the environment (the market) because they can actively seek their prey (prospecting), develop a strategy to "attack" the prey and close on them - bringing them back to the home base. Hunters are not dependent on the environment - they actively adjust to the environment in which they are and control their activity to maximise the opportunities.

Farmers starve (read go out of business) because of their inability to harvest a crop (i.e., the phone doesn't ring!). Hunters only starve if they don't go out and pursue prey - it's the hunter's choice. This should describe why the skill sets for "hunters" are dramatically different from those of "farmers." Can "farmers" be taught to be "hunters?" In many cases yes — in others, no. However, every farmer deserves to be presented with the skill sets required to become a "hunter" and survive in a difficult environment. However, not all of them will pick up the tools and use them.

The following are some of the skill sets of "hunters" that can be broken down into specific training bytes:

New Business Development or Locating the "Prey." In the current hotel environment, some markets that were previously lucrative have diminished in volume. The corporate and association markets being two of these. This doesn't mean that there is not business to be had from these segments, but identifying where takes more time and strategy. This is a "hunter" skill that can be trained. The "hunter" also needs to identify different types of "prey" - those market segments that are less easy to locate and close but who are still relatively plentiful.

Developing the Strategy. There are several stages to this one but the first begins with research. A recent seminar participant said that she had begun researching a market segment but that it takes a great deal of time. It does - but this puts her way ahead of others who haven't begun the process. Smart hunters know that their chances of success improve when they research at which watering hole their prey is most likely to be and develop a strategy versus the hunters who simply spot a prey and charge, often unable to outrun the prey itself. The approach follows from the research and adds significantly to the success rate.

Closing on the Prey. Okay, this is where the analogy breaks down a bit. We want this to be pleasant experience for our "prey" to not only survive but also benefit from what the hotel has to offer. This includes the qualifying, presenting and closing stages. Building the relationship is also part of this stage.

It is also my observation that potential sales "hunters" are often frustrated by the attitudes of managers who are still operating in the paradigm that hotel sales people are essentially farmers. These managers are still operating on the assumptions that hotel sales is revenue management versus revenue generation. The skill set exercise is one that both can use.

Security in Hotels Sales

The threat of looming war is taking an already elevated level of security to new heights. Public buildings, office towers and military installations are increasingly difficult to access. Hotels, especially large destination and gateway properties, are aware of the potential risks to guests and have their own security issues. This is likely to become more of an issue when and if the US goes to war in Iraq. The temptation on the part of hoteliers may be similar to that following September 11. Immediately following that event most businesses, including hotels and hotel companies, went into a temporary state of paralysis. Business travel came to a screeching halt and hoteliers' first reaction was to look for ways to reduce expenses.

However, this time expenses have already been cut to the bone in many cases. There are some hotels and hotel companies that included the marketing and sales function in their expense revisions. While there was often a great deal of 'flab' in these budgeted expenses, the smart companies measured their cuts against productivity and many have sought to provide enhanced training opportunities for their sales staff to enable them to cope with the new economic realty.

When we look at the travel trends following September 11, we see that corporations have pared down their business travel - this will be attenuated with the threat of terrorism again on US soil. Association and trade show attendance has been negatively impacted by the economy. The market segments that were once the backbone of hotel revenues can no longer be assumed to support property budgets.

Couple that increased level of security with the urgent need on the part of hotels to develop new business, a new approach to prospecting for new business has to be developed. A mainstay of 'backyard' marketing used to be to make cold calls on every commercial building within a certain radius. This simply will no longer work in major metropolitan areas. Access will be denied very quickly to those without appointments. Alternative markets take more time, skill and creativity to develop.

How then to ensure that a hotel is squeezing every bit of business out of their local markets? The following are but a few ideas and certainly not exhaustive.

— *Develop and maintain a directory of businesses and associations in your market.* If you have compiled a Territory Report in the past, you have a head start. If not, there are many business directories that you can buy. However, remember that once these directories are published, they are going out of date. Be sure to check the publication date so that you are not buying more directory information than you need. Go for a drive and walk into buildings. Write down the list of business and organisations on the inside directory so that you have an up to date list.

— *Research which industry sectors are outperforming the market.* There is still corporate business out there, you will need to discover which industry sectors are thriving in this economy and go after them. An excellent tool for this is USA Today's weekly stock market sector report that tells you which industries as a whole are outperforming the market.

— *Cross-reference the sector list against the directory.* This will tell you the prospects in your market that in all likelihood are doing well and can pay your rate. The professional associations that serve these sectors are also likely to have strong attendance. For example, the pharmaceutical and medical supply sectors are performing reasonably well. Apart from the obvious, calling any pharmaceutical companies in your market, visit your local hospital and ask the purchasing department who their suppliers are and can you get a list or offer them a rate for those suppliers coming into town.

— *Explore alternative markets.* Why we dump the SMERF market on the newest sales manager or the sales assistant. More than ever, this market requires a lot of creative 'digging' to uncover groups that you may have never considered before.

These are just a very few of the things that hotels can do to redirect their sales efforts for new business development. Communicating with and qualifying these new leads also requires a different strategy than what has always been done before.

Revenue Recovery

Many General Managers and Directors of Sales establish sales goals for their sales teams that are not being met. They indicate that they cannot seem to get their sales people to develop new business and close it, despite the resources that management is making available to them. The sales people are not sure how to accomplish the things that they are being asked to do.

There is no doubt that it is tough out there but the strong sales people will not only succeed but regard this as an opportunity to prove something to themselves and their management. Sales people with the 'right stuff' want to know how to develop their skills. The others spend their time figuring out why these things won't and can't work.

The skill set that made sales people successful during the boom years is not necessarily the skill set that will help them succeed during the tough times. When all that was required was to answer the phone, follow-up and book the business, the expectations were different. As a respected business associate put it so well, "What we had were farmers who harvested the field, what we need now are hunters to locate and close in on new business."

Not everyone is capable of making the transition from 'farmer' to 'hunter'. Some will pick up the tools of the new skill set and embrace the transition; others will simply not be capable of doing that. The onus is on management to ascertain who in their department will make the cut and how to hire those who have it in them to become hunters. It all goes back to having the right people in the right positions if you want to succeed. In other words, it all boils down to the point of hire. General Managers who assumed their positions during the mid-nineties often don't know what to look for in a potential candidate. Experience in the past is not necessarily a predictor of success in this economy.

The interview process can be very subjective. It is unfortunate but those people are being set up to fail and it is not their fault – it was bad 'hire' for which management needs to take responsibility. Here are a few steps that managers can take and tools that you can use to make the best possible hiring decisions. They are not infallible but can be predictors of success for hiring good sales people:

Personality Inventories: Decide the specific traits that you are looking for in a successful sales person who can work well in your organisation.

Questions to ask. Give careful thought to the questions that you are going to ask a candidate. These should include specific questions regarding successes and challenges. "What was the most difficult selling situation you have encountered and how did you handle it?" Solicit the input of your staff and other successful sales people into the development of your list of questions. Make sure that you ask the same questions to all potential candidates so you have a basis for comparison and write down the answers. Good sales people overcome obstacles in their personal and professional lives in order to be successful.

Involve others in the process. Have other department heads interview the potential candidate as well as someone in your sales department with whom this candidate will have to work. Record their input in the interview file. This also puts the interview process into perspective and allows some objectivity.

Can they sell you? Put yourself in the place of the decision maker at one of your accounts. Who are they and how will they react to this person? Does this person project the skills to connect, establish rapport and build a relationship with the contacts at the accounts and in the market that you are considering them for?

Never make a decision based on one interview. No matter how desperate you are to fill a position, take your time. Call them back for at least a second if not a third interview. This gives you an idea of whether or not they have more than one suit. It also allows you time to think and view them over a period of time. The 'aura' that they may have projected on the first interview may not be as glowing the third time that you see them. Let them know your time frame for making this decision.

Make the expectations for the position perfectly clear. Do not underestimate the difficulty of the position or the market. Let them know what you expect in terms of booking activity, call goals and follow-up. Give them an incentive to run for and how you will schedule regular reviews to evaluate their skills and progress. Also, outline the potential consequences of not achieving their objectives.

While the above are not the only things to consider, it is a good guideline to use in the interview process. Once you have hired a candidate, treat them well and give them the tools to do their job. Provide training and an orientation programme to acquaint them with the property's operation. Have them spend time in each department (yes, include housekeeping and maintenance). The responsibility of hiring well is yours.

Changing Rules in Hotel Sales

Once upon a time not too long ago, prior to September 11, hotel sales in a limited service environment was reasonably straightforward. PKF was anticipating that this sector would be the ultimate beneficiary of the economic downturn as customers traded into this sector from the higher rated full service, mid-market and luxury sectors. At the time this was written, in late August, the limited service and all-suite sectors were expected to maintain their profit levels in 2001. The rules have changed.

Until now, limited service hotels experienced a slight decrease in demand in most markets but not stunningly in relation to their full service competitors. Many limited serve hotels did not use a sales person, rather the GM, who had absolutely nothing else to do, was expected to function as the sales person as well. In those situations where there was a sales person, it was usually someone with limited sales experience, perhaps promoted from the front desk. The most common reasons for this was the position was not very well paid and the job market was so tight that it was virtually impossible to attract someone with sales or hotel credentials at that salary. The rules have changed.

The GM who never had time in the first place now has less time as many hotels have cut staff to respond to the dramatic drop in occupancy. While this may be somewhat shortsighted, it is the GM who is picking up the slack at the front desk and performing front office procedures. There is no way that the GM has the time to contact all of the accounts and ascertain the conditions of the changes in their travel policies, their new rate sensitivity and what it would take to get what little remains of their business.

In an environment where the rules have changed, the temptation on the part of owners and management companies is to hunker down - slash the staff to the bone, eliminate all sales and promotion expense and let the salaried managers pick up the difference by working additional hours. Those hotels that have been operating a flabby organisation may benefit in the short term but it is not the strategy that will position a hotel to survive and succeed in the next six to nine months of uncertainty and potential recession.

Make no mistake - there will be winners and losers in this new environment. The parameters of success for the winners won't be as grand as they were a brief twelve months ago but the penalties for the losers never change. Erosion of the asset and the ultimate penalty, foreclosure, is the consequence of short-term thinking. Formulate a strategy based on possible scenarios.

Many hotels did not adequately track where their business was coming from in the past when demand was high. Those hotels have a steeper learning curve than those who had the foresight to use the tracking capabilities in their franchise reservations systems. Do not ask the GM to perform this function - it is not going to happen! If you have a sales person, be very specific about the direction you want them to take, the deals they can cut. If you don't have a sales person, get one or contract to a sales and marketing person who will perform this function for you in the short term, like the next six to nine months until things stabilise. The benefit of the latter option is that you incur no payroll burden and you can hire more expertise than you could afford long-term.

With the airline industry laying off so many customer service associates, it is an excellent time to hire people with experience and personality. It is an opportunity to eliminate those GSAs that were hired because they fogged the mirror — the ones who couldn't be bothered smiling at a guest or making eye contact. Invest in some short-term training to upgrade the skills of the sales and customer service staff. If you can't afford to hire experience, train the staff you can afford. This is an investment you can't afford not to make. Find training that produces results tailored for your situation. It can be seminars or distance learning that does not require time away from the property or the job.

The winners under the new rules will be those that resisted the urge to react with short-term thinking. The winners will be the ones who positioned themselves for the future and not just reacted to the immediate situation. People will travel again by air and by car. Their requirements of us do not change - a good product and good service at a fair price.

General Manager's Role in Sales

Some companies already have that position and most should, especially now that the economy is dictating a move away from accounting driven corporate cultures to sales driven cultures. Most hotels went on 'auto pilot' when the summer season approached and made certain that the revenue management systems were in place to maximise the revenues generated by peak demand.

While the General Manager has always been the CEO of their hotel – to their staff and to their customers — most have yet to truly use the power of the position effectively to promote sales and assume the role of CMO. General Managers who rose through the ranks on the operations side are now under increasing pressure from their corporate office to become actively involved in the sales effort. GMs that assumed their positions during the 'boom' years excel at revenue management but are unsure how to support and monitor the sales effort. Those that remember the last economic downturn have in many cases forgotten how to do that.

However, several large new companies had moved into the area and the increase in corporate demand should have more than compensated for the decrease in leisure. This GM had attended the luncheon, received the report but the information obviously didn't pass it to sales as all of the sales efforts were still being directed at wholesalers and tour operators. The moral of the story is to check the content of the call reports not just the number of calls.

Market intelligence or Market IQ is something that the GM is in a unique position to gather. Do you:

— Attend planning and zoning meetings

— Schmooze the Economic Development people (they do use your hotel when they bring in prospective company's executives, don't they?)

— Participate actively in industry associations

— Browse the business section of your local paper every day – bankruptcies generate a lot of business

— Visit your fellow GMs and make a mental note of who is doing business at their hotel that day
— Network with consultants (like me) and the business reporters of your local papers to get a broad overview of the market

Measuring Effectiveness of Hotel Sales

Often management does not closely monitor sales effectiveness when things are going reasonably well. When demand is high and the issue is one of managing the yield, sales departments can become confused as to the goals ("Do you want the business or not?") and management is often less than clear on tying yield management goals to sales production goals and incentives. Sales people, sensitive as they are, become discouraged by what they perceive as mixed messages on rate versus occupancy.

There are three distinct areas that can assist management in measuring sales effectiveness;

— Defining the areas to be evaluated;
— Monitoring sales performance in relation to the above areas and
— Designing incentives to reflect Management's goals for the property.

Defining the Areas of Evaluation

— How do you set sales goals? Do you establish call quotas or revenue quotas based on the success of top line room revenue in relation to budget and last year? The fatal flaw with call quotas is that they are easy to fudge (not that anyone on your staff would ever do that) and a lot of calls made without enthusiasm or with poor sales skills fulfills the quota but does nothing for the property's revenue.

— What reports are you requesting from your sales people? The reports that you request communicate to them what is important to you. If you are asking for raw numbers of calls without any information on who was called and why, you are not getting the whole picture.

— The next one is tricky but evaluating sales activity in relation to potential revenue is critical to maximise productivity. For example, is too much time being spent on developing low-rated contract or SMERF business when the denials reflect higher rated demand is being lost? Have you targeted the market segments most likely to give you business at the higher rate and restructured the department's market segments and time allocations accordingly?

Monitoring Areas of Sales Performance.

— When a sales person comes victoriously into the office or calls to announce a great piece of business that has been booked, do you ask how this lead was generated – did we develop it or was it an inquiry? One reflects skill, the other order taking.

— Are you assessing the mix of calls? How many are calls to new prospects, how many are routine traces, how many are outside calls? Of those that are traces, where in the sales 'pipeline' are they – at the qualifying stage, negotiating the contract or closing?

— Do you spot-check weekly reports? There is story about Curt Carlson, founder of Carlson companies, that may be apocryphal but is a shrewd lesson for all managers to learn. It is said that when he held meetings with his division heads, he asked them to bring their P&Ls on overheads. He would then project them on a screen and pick several line items at random on each sheet and inquire as to what that number represented. His logic was that if a division head could explain everything that was in that number, they knew what was in the rest of their P&L. Do you routinely pick items at random on the sales reports and inquire as to how we got that prospect, what went on during that call and where we stand with that prospect?

Designing Incentives to Reflect Management Goals

— Is your sales department responsible for total room revenue of the property including transient and group? If not, they may overbook group blocks at the expense of transient to fulfill their group goals.

— Does your sales incentive programme reflect your fluctuating seasonal goals, higher rates when demand warrants and higher volume in the off seasons? Sales was booking a large volume of group business in summer at significantly less than rack rate. An examination of the incentive programme revealed that the sales incentive plan was based on annualised group revenue and the demand for group rooms was significantly higher in the summer than in the winter. Therefore, if the sales department was going to make bonus they had to 'make hay' while the sun shone in the summer. By re-weighting the sales incentive programme so that group rooms booked for the summer months account for a smaller percentage of their annual bonus with a much higher percentage for group business booked in the winter, they are able to re-direct their efforts and benefit both themselves and the property's goals.

The urgency for measuring sales effectiveness when demand is high may seem to be misplaced but is your hotel doing as well as it could be doing? Remember, a rising tide floats all boats and when the tide begins to go out (winter is coming and so perhaps, are new hotels in your market), it is those properties with sharp sales efforts and the methods for measuring that performance that will thrive.

Hotel Sales Training

The current employment climate in the hotel industry has put severe limitations on the ability of hotels to recruit and retain sales people with sales experience and/or a background in hotels. In many cases, we are promoting from within, usually the front desk, or relying on intuition that untried recruits are trainable. This situation is even more apparent in the limited to moderate service sectors, that is, non-convention hotels reliant on their local markets to generate the majority of their demand.

Compounding the situation in the limited and moderate service sectors are decreasing occupancies in both the limited service and all suite sectors for 1999. This makes an effective sales effort more critical at a time when flat revenues limit the resources a property or management company has to retain qualified sales and marketing professionals.

In the current climate, we are dealing with sales people often with no experience, whose longevity with the property is relatively brief, often only nine to eighteen months. With little training and a steep learning curve, it becomes the 'deep end of the pool' training. That is, we throw them into the deep end of the pool and wait on the side. If they float, we figure they will make it. The other side of the coin is that with such a short average duration on the job, many companies are reluctant to spend the dollars sending them to training.

With a high degree of turnover and a shortage of recruits, sales positions, both at the property and corporate levels are left open for long periods of time. Any sales momentum is lost and clients have difficulty being serviced. In addition, many 'experienced' sales people were never taught the basic steps of the sales process or how to completely penetrate their markets.

Understanding what new sales people are looking for from an employment situation is crucial to maximising both longevity and training. Studies show that they are not there for the money alone, and we all know that the salaries in the hotel sales field have not kept pace with the rest of the marketplace. On the one hand, they want to feel part of a team, that their input and opinions are solicited and valued but on the other, they want to know what's in it for them, in terms of rewards for performance and career potential. When an inexperienced recruit is left untrained, they become frustrated and are easy prey for the competition or other industries.

As well, clients have become fickle and, with overbuilding in this sector, will switch to a new hotel for a few dollars less in rate or a newer hotel product with additional amenities such as a two room suite for the price of a room at a traditional property. They have also become cynical about building relationships with sales people due to the turnover factor. The days are also gone when most companies can drive all of their business to one hotel. Their employees are demanding more flexibility based on their preferences and frequent guest programmes, when location and rate are relatively similar. The traditional 'booker' now exerts influence but can not always guarantee the choices that an employee will make.

It is now more important than ever to 'spread the risk' of losing revenue from several key accounts to a total market penetration strategy that includes smaller companies which, if the company's fortunes change, will not take the hotel's revenue base down with it. One need look no further than the Seattle area when Boeing was downsizing and restructuring to see an example of an entire market's dependency on one key account. Those hotels that had built a broad customer base fared better than those that didn't.

An examination of a hotel's source of business report usually reveals that while a few accounts can be identified that produce a large number of rooms, it is usually no more than 15 to 20% of a hotel's occupied rooms, the majority of the rest being frequent guest programmes or unidentified 'corporate' and 'discount'. The old 80/20 rule does not necessarily apply anymore. In a corporate market, up to 80% of your business now comes from 'independents', employees of larger companies that when location is equal will stay where their frequent guest points are and contractors and consultants who will make their own decisions based on the same factors. The 'independent' client is difficult to identify and woo but not impossible.

Reducing the learning curve and enabling sales people to generate revenue for the hotel in the shortest period of time is the goal of effective training and should be conducted as soon as possible following the recruitment of a new sales person. Whether training occurs in a seminar setting or one-on-one, results should be tangible in terms of a sales person's immediate effectiveness and quantifiable in terms of additional revenue generation within 60 days after it is completed. It should include on-going reinforcement through the Internet (this is the dot.com generation) or, if unavailable, more traditional methods such as conference calls and availability to counsel via e-mail or telephone. A newsletter with concrete sales 'tools' that sales people can implement keeps the basic concepts fresh in their minds.

Those hotels and management companies that take training seriously can reduce turnover and retain staff longer than the average. Recruitment and retention will continue to be a problem for the foreseeable future, which is why training needs to be ongoing and constantly reinforced. The General Managers need to be included in the process as often they are the only ones on property to sell and have the responsibility of overseeing the sales effort every day. Incentives for sales and GMs based on property revenue keeps everyone focused on the goal.

8

Challenges of Revenue Management

In a typical urban/suburban mid level corporate transient property, the mid-week peaks are dominated by business travelers whose rate sensitivity is less as they, individually, are not paying the bill. Another factor to consider is that bookings from all electronic sources have increased another 30-40% from 2003. This includes all channels from the GDS systems, e-commerce channels and the franchise web site. These bookings are also driven by an increase in leisure travel that has been induced by the lowest airfares in a decade. While airfares remain low, this segment demonstrated in the summer of 2004 that they were willing to pay higher hotel rates than in past years.

The dilemma for hotel sales departments is to locate and manage group business to fill in the blanks mid-week and weekends, often from market segments and demand generators that press for lower rates. They also are dealing with third party meeting planners attempting to negotiate the best (read lowest) rates for their clients.

The Revenue Manager is pressing for a higher rate, group booking contacts are pressing for lower rates and the sales person is under pressure to meet their booking goals — it is a stressful situation for the sales department! The solutions are varied but hinge upon the ability of the sales person and department to understand and be able to measure the impact of potential bookings and rates upon the hotel's revenue management strategy. Once they understand those parameters, they can then align their new business development activities in relation to the client profiles that fit the revenue management model.

It is both the lack of understanding and/or the inability to measure their potential contracts prior to negotiating and booking that provokes the criticism that "sales only wants to book the lowest rates." My firm belief is that they will stand their ground if given the tools in order to, first of all, develop new business in line with the revenue management strategy and secondly, measure the value of a group to the hotel's top line. In other words, understand the difference between good business and bad.

Revenue Management Strategy

Those who are involved in developing the strategy have "buy in" to its successful execution. A hotel company has taken the position that they want to reduce the number of locally negotiated rate contracts and increase the rate on the remaining ones in order to drive a higher ADR in the mid-week period which is the period of the greatest ADR potential. Sales is fine with the understanding that their ADRs for groups during the weekends will remain the same as the past year and maybe even be a bit reduced in order to attract SMERFE business. It is a deal that is cut so that everyone knows what the expectations are. The Revenue Manager is part of the sales team rather than a direct report to the Rooms Division.

Develop Client Profiles for Each Rate Period. In order to be more effective in locating prospects that will fit into the management, it is imperative to know what you are looking for. In other words, which types of groups in market segments and sub segments will fit within the rate and catering parameters that will align with the revenue management strategy. Attempting to meet these goals through only responding to telephone inquiries and working the trace files is insufficient to attain the goals. First of all, there is no control over the kind of prospects calling and the pressure builds to respond to their requests if this is your only means of prospecting. Secondly, the accounts in the trace files may or may not be in alignment with the new revenue goals in terms of rates and meeting configurations.

A client profile should be driven by market segment, where the bookings are likely to originate, their rate sensitivity or history and their meeting configurations. For example, in the SMERFE market, a group of wine enthusiasts may be less rate sensitive and more inclined to spend money on F&B than a group of students. A group originating in a city with a higher ADR may be less rate sensitive than those that originate locally.

Develop a New Business Development Strategy. Once the client profiles are developed, it becomes a matter of developing a strategy to locate and qualify these prospects. Strategies might include using the Internet to locate certain organisations within a market segment from a specific geographic location or getting on an email distribution list or mailing list for organisations that have the potential to produce groups for the hotel is another one. There are web sites that specialise in producing leads for groups for hotels in various market segments. These can be sorted by geographic location and often give the rates, meeting specs and history of where the group last met. No strategy is complete without an action plan for implementation.

Provide a Group Revenue Management Tool. A revenue management tool can be as simple as a spreadsheet of the group rooms budget by month into which the parameters of the group can be entered so that the sales person can see how the number of rooms at the proposed rate effects the room revenue of the entire hotel for the period. It can be as sophisticated as a computer program that measures the revenue of a group on all profit centers. These take various forms and often are included with the sales contact management system such as the ones offered by Delphi. Some of these products interface with the property's PMS and Revenue management systems.

The future of the hotel sales is in being able to first of all, locate groups that fit the revenue management strategy and secondly, measure the viability of a group in the date ranges and rate requested in relation to the hotel's revenue management strategy.

Processes and Functionality

There are a variety of issues that affect the functionality of these processes online. Many of the tools are inexpensive and easy to accomplish — we need to expand the notion of how we conduct sales to include online tools as standard operational processes

New Business Development. There are a variety of online resources available to the sales department, many by market segment. The sales department needs to be working these with the same intensity that they work trace files. If your sales department isn't making these a vital component of their prospecting activity, you can be sure that other hotels are — and gaining market share from these sites.

Pre-Approach Qualifying. There is so much information on the web — at the click of a mouse. The sales staff should be accessing information about their prospects prior to contact so that they know if they are worth pursuing. They need to know which factors to look for in reports that indicate the potential of a prospect to produce and to make a judgment about those in which they should be investing their time.

Using E-Postcards. E-postcards can be created quickly and effectively at a desktop PC. Their uses span individual prospect approaches to creating targeted e-blasts that fly under the radar of spamming. A little creativity and basic computer skills are all that are required.

E-flyers. These range from the extremely clever to the purely informative. They make an excellent vehicle for customer relationship management and to inform a broad range of guests and clients, who have given permission to receive them, of changes at the hotel and special promotions.

E-stationary. Make your hotel's email correspondence from all departments stand apart from the rest of the hotel e-chatter that hits your clients' Inbox! This can be designed to have the same look and feel as the web site and online brochures (you do have online brochures, don't you?)

E-brochures. While printed brochures are not quite yet dinosaurs, how many do you have left in your hotel supply closet from the 50,000 that you ordered prior to the new renovation and addition of high-speed Internet access to your amenity list? At a panel discussion of meeting planners, they all indicated that they have cleaned out or eliminated their massive file cabinets full of hotel sales kits. The meeting planners unanimously agreed that they would prefer to have brochures and sales kits electronically so that they can be downloaded as needed.

The Web Site. All too often the web site is developed without the input of sales or consideration of how it can be used as a sales tool — not just a design masterpiece. The inclusion of design elements and photography that appeals across and to many market segments makes it more functional for the generation of group leads. Franchise web sites offer the opportunity to include multiple photos but many hotels only include the exterior and maybe one other photo! The description screens are rarely edited to reflect seasonality and special packages. The reservation function is awkward at best — at worst it doesn't interface with the property management system.

GM'S Role in Revenue Management

Revenue Manager actually did all day to viewing the Revenue Manager as setting policy on the rates to be quoted by everyone in a position to do so — with a lot of comments in between. Some viewed the Revenue Manager as a gatherer of data only and the position as being essentially a part-time function while others viewed the Revenue Manager as critical to the overall revenue strategy of the hotel.

The relationship between the sales department of the hotel and the Revenue Manager is another potential area of confusion. In some situations, Directors of Sales have indicated that there was little communication between the two departments. Many times group blocks were sabotaged by a lower rate that the Revenue Manager had offered to the Electronic Distribution Channels, incurring a high attrition rate for groups whose attendees had located that lower rate for the hotel on the Internet and booked out of the block.

One DOS indicated that her staff had to get approval from the Revenue Manager prior to quoting rates for groups. It was often difficult for the sales person to explain a lower rate quote for a certain period of time justified by the organisation's potential to book more business in an opportunity period, the need for rate consistency within a market segment, or a long standing relationship that the organisation had with the hotel.

How does a GM lead the Revenue Management process to ensure that both the needs of the client and the hotel's revenue objectives are met, not to mention ensure the cohesiveness of the team?

Understand the Revenue Management Process. Many General Mangers are uncomfortable with the process because they simply do not fully understand it. The discipline of revenue management has morphed over time with many new systems and programmes available. Take a course on up to date revenue management. There are many offered on the Internet that are both time and cost effective. You cannot manage the process unless you fully understand it.

Develop an open attitude about the Electronic Distribution Channels. Back off, take a deep breath and consider the following: 1. These are reservations that your front desk or reservations staff does not have to process, 2. You have been paying a commission to Travel Agents since the beginning of time anyway and 3. You don't have to offer them a dirt bag rate! While recently assisting a client in the development of the hotel's revenue management strategy, it became evident that the ADR for these channels in one high occupancy period exceeded the hotel's ADR by $5 (after commission). Why? Because the hotel had let them pull the rate from the GDS during a period when all low rates were closed. By understanding this, you can make these electronic channels a valuable part of your revenue management strategy.

Establish a Revenue Management Strategy. Simply put, this means establishing room and rate allocations by market segment and opportunity dates and seasonality for the year, to be reviewed quarterly. This should be an essential part of the marketing plan developed in collaboration with the Revenue Manager, the sales department, front office and reservation managers and anyone else whose department is affected. Be prepared for heated discussions as everyone makes their case for their "pet" market segments. Make it clear that if sales or anyone else wants to give a lower rate to a group or segment in a given time period, the revenue must be made up in other segments.

Conflict Management. Expect conflict. Create a framework for managing revenue management conflicts when they arise and establish a decision making process — even if that means that you cast the deciding vote.

Be prepared to take risks. Revenue Management is not an exact science. Be prepared to take risks yourself and encourage the "risk takers" on your staff, provided that they can provide valid reasons to take them. You will win sometimes and sometimes you will lose. A General Manager decided to vote against becoming a host hotel for a certain group and not to offer the preferred rate with the comp rooms that the group was asking for. His was the only hotel in the market not to do so. The "last to fill at the highest rate" strategy is always a risky one. A week prior to the group's arrival, they were sitting pretty much dead empty, the anticipated demand no where in sight and the GM was sweating bullets. At the end of the day, or night in this case, the hotel filled at a rate $25 higher than the rest of the market but it could have gone either way.

Leading the revenue management process is critical to the success of the hotel. It is not about analysing the data within the spreadsheet but is ultimately about creating value for guests in every market segment without jeopardising the hotel's revenue goals — it is that guest value quotient that we often lose site of in the process!

A revenue management strategy that incorporates all of the revenue drivers such as GDS, the web site and the electronic distribution channels is key. However, it requires the involvement of the sales department and all other profit centers of the hotel. This is unlike a budget in that a revenue strategy is renewable and adjustable where a budget is usually written in stone.

A sound revenue management strategy includes the optimum revenue mix and the tactics to achieve it — this is where the marketing plan comes in! "Managing" revenue is just that — it assumes an element of control in the revenue that you accept from various sources based upon cost of reservation, commissions, etc.

A revenue management strategy establishes "target" numbers to be achieved through a variety of ways; sales, manipulating the GDS, controlling the allocation and rate in the electronic distribution channels, etc. In other words, it is a pro-active rather than reactive function that simply turns the faucets on and off.

The sales strategies in the marketing plan flow from the revenue management strategy although sales is critical in developing it. The sales department is critical in that they have their fingers on the pulse of the market. They are responsible for assembling the economic information on market conditions and analysing the potential threats to the market as well as identifying the opportunities. The sales department knows the potential of each market segment and the rate that each one will bear.

The development of the revenue management strategy allows sales to gage how many rooms in a given period they can book by market segment and at what rate. It also insures that existing and future group blocks won't be sabotaged by lower rates on the web site or distribution channels.

How exactly should this process work?

Gathering the info: Each member of the team, but especially sales, should have been keeping information in regard to the market such as trends indicated by the STR reports and other industry sources. Sales should take the temperature of top accounts to see what their forecasts for travel next year look like. The group logs pace reports for this year and next year should also be put into the file. Sales should also have the situation analysis completed as well as identified challenges and opportunities for the upcoming year.

Analysing the Revenue Data: The revenue reports should be analysed to indicate the percentages currently generated by all revenue drivers. This, of course assumes that the data is accurate. If anyone has any doubts about the importance of proper market segment coding by reservations and the front desk they should end here. It is "GIGO" (garbage in — garbage out)! If there aren't accurate numbers, you will be playing a SWAG game.

The Facilitation: This is the meeting of the minds, GM, sales, reservations and any other interested party such as the owner. They take a look at the budget, market conditions, all sources of revenue, etc. and begin projecting the revenue strategy by segment. This can be a contentious process as the sales department fights for accounts and room allocations by rate. However, as an associate once said, harmony is vastly overrated. This process can take several days as all of the evidence is presented and numbers are plugged into the model and adjusted — yada, yada. It never hurts to have an outside consultant facilitate this process to provide objective third party input.

The Final Product: The spreadsheet, created from compromise that fulfills the requirement of the budget, becomes the basis of the revenue strategy. Every revenue driver is identified and the ideal mix of revenue and rate is there to yield the targeted REVPAR. Every revenue driver in the revenue strategy should have its own strategy and tactics section in the marketing plan — including the web site, the GDS strategy and the electronic distribution channels (don't make the mistake of leaving it up to the franchise).

The Review Process: The same fractious group that designed the strategy should meet periodically, it could be monthly or quarterly, to make adjustments based upon reality. In the initial development, "triggers" should have been identified that would automatically call for adjustments. Those triggers include unanticipated market changes, good or bad, changes in the economy and any national security breaches.

It's a "messy" process, but a necessary one for the marketing plan to be developed. It then becomes the road map for the coming year. The marketing plan is not just about sales but the revenue management strategy for the entire hotel.

Integration of Revenue Drivers

As peak season nears for many hotels, revenue management is the key to a successful summer season. Leisure remains strong even as business travel continues to disappoint and it is imperative that in March the pieces are in place to maximise revenue. Potential customers are much smarter than they used to be about locating, qualifying and making their hotel choice. In many cases, this process is completed without ever contacting the hotel.

Revenue drivers are defined as all areas of revenue generation within the organisation. This includes central reservations, property-level reservations, the sales department, the electronic distribution channels and the web site. While franchised properties have a higher level of consistency through the GDS, it still requires monitoring and management at the company or property levels.

At a recent sales seminar, participants expressed frustration that they are largely unaware of, nor are they consulted about the rates that are posted on the electronic distribution channels. One result is a very high attrition rate in meetings and conventions as attendees book their hotel at these lower rates and "fall" off the group block. Another consequence is when the rate posted is lower than what has been negotiated with third-party suppliers such as wholesalers.

A coaching client of mine expressed frustration over his lack of consultation in the development of the new property web site and the rates that are being quoted through the site. First of all, the content was skewed to a specific market segment that was not representative of the core business segment and secondly, the copy changes disrupted the optimisation strategy.

Secondly, the rates that were quoted were not at all aligned with the rates being quoted at the property level or through the central reservations agent and many room descriptions were inaccurate. The end result was that not only was this hotel nowhere to be found on the key word searches in the major search engines — a potential disaster for this independent property, but fewer reservations were being made through the site.

Collaboration across all departments that generate revenue is the only way to ensure continuity. This need not be a tedious process of endless meetings. A few things put into place and adjusted periodically, based on market conditions and forecasts, are sufficient:

— *Product/Rate Positioning:* A plan for product/rate positioning is ideally developed as part of the Business/Marketing plan process and includes consideration of the product/rate positioning of the competitive set, group bookings, rate resistance input from reservations and past history. Once the strategy is developed, it then only needs to be adjusted periodically. Don't forget to monitor the franchise yield management system in light of groups or events in previous years that may not be a factor in the present year.

— *Existing and Anticipated Contracts:* These include group contracts, volume contracts with LNRs, wholesalers and any other rate commitments. Just as the sales department makes decisions based on the rate structure, so should consideration be given to any agreements made thorough sales. It is one thing to adjust rates on the web site or distribution channels to drive volume at a slow time but if it undermines the agreements above, it is counter productive.

— *Web Site Presence and Reservations:* Many leisure customers locate the hotel through key word searches on the search engines. Others locate the hotel on the electronic distribution channels then access the hotel's proprietary web site. Still others will pick up the phone after visiting both and call reservations to see if they can cut a better deal. It is essential that the "message" of rate and offering be relatively consistent across all channels to be effective. The rates on the web site need to be adjusted in tandem with the electronic distribution channels and reservations needs to be aware of what's appearing on both.

Another consideration in web site development is the increased use of the site as a sales tool. It becomes the electronic brochure. The sales department's inclusion in its development is essential to the site's secondary role as the electronic brochure. Sales people should be accessing the site with their clients to moderate the virtual tour. If there is a special rate posted that is inconsistent with the rates sales are quoting, it blows them out of the water and appears to the client that the hotel doesn't know what it is doing.

The process of collecting the information is about communication and collaboration and can be accomplished through periodic updates from the revenue drivers to the revenue management team. This swings both ways as revenue management needs to keep the revenue drivers informed of their proposed tactics in order to solicit input and buy in.

The consequence of not doing this is to present an inconsistent message to the public who is in the position of making selections without any direct contact with the property thus depriving the hotel from any opportunity to make adjustments or explain the disconnect. In the consumer's mind, a hotel that can't get its act together to project consistent rates may have the same problem when it comes to servicing them as guests. The issue is more than rate parity, it is aligning the rate structures between all revenue generating departments so that each is maximising their contribution to revenue.

Revenue Management in Today's Market

Oct 29, 2001 - Prior to September 11, hotels worldwide were feeling the effects of an economic softening. Although industry analysts were forecasting decreased RevPAR, in the post-911 era, hotels have experienced unprecedented challenges in managing their businesses.

Automated revenue management (RM) solutions provide hotels with sustainable competitive advantages to navigate through this period of uncertainty. These solutions provide quantifiable financial and operational benefits in all market conditions, critical to the success and longevity of hotel properties worldwide.

Automated RM solutions successfully assist hotels in optimising demand and increasing RevPAR. Booking controls such as rate availability, overbooking controls and length-of-stay restrictions are designed to accept the right mix of business, at the best rate, at the right time for the optimal length of stay. Revenue management results have been impressive; occupancies have increased as well average daily rates with measurable RevPAR increases.

The question today is do automated RM solutions provide benefits in a soft market? The answer is a resounding yes. Here are a few examples of how automated RM systems provide hotels with tangible benefits and sustainable competitive advantages.

Hotels with automated RM solutions continue to outperform other hotels in their markets, even in periods of declining demand. According Universal Orlando, "Universal has seen growth in a market that is down, some of it is certainly attributable to revenue management."

The fact remains that the economy works in cycles – up and down and up and down again. Automated RM solutions do their best, most valuable work when demand is fluctuating between busy and not-so-busy nights, not just when hotels are sure to always fill up. These solutions generally outperform manual environments, semi-automated tools and decision support systems by 4 to 12%. Detailed analytical processes, scientific forecasting, automated restrictions and constant monitoring, combine to ensure hotels receive unequalled benefits. In all market conditions, hotels with automated RM solutions will maintain significant advantages over their competition.

By harnessing the power of the microchip these solutions efficiently analyse massive amounts of data picking up even slight changes in demand. In times of less than anticipated demand, this information becomes strategically important, enabling properties with information to deploy sales and marketing strategies to build demand.

When demand fluctuates and is uncertain, automated RM solutions continue to deploy decisions to optimise both occupancy and rates. Even in environments of low demand where occupancy could be as low as 30%, there are often special events, holidays and perhaps trade events that present significant opportunities to increase revenue.

Take for example events such as ITB/Berlin, the London Trade Show, Paris Air Show, Comdex or the Bledisloe Cup Match and Communiqué Asia; each of these events presents an important opportunity to increase revenue. According to Vail Resorts, one of the largest resort operators in North America, "The most critical factors that contribute to successful room yielding are: maximising occupancies; booking guests with the longer length of stays; managing the amount of overbooking we are willing to accept; and selling rooms at the best price based on demand. That's why we chose..a system with an automatic, integrated decision-making ability to consider those factors at the moment when reservations are made."

In difficult times, properties often cut back staff or staffing hours resulting in increased workloads for those who remain. Automated RM solutions represent a radical reduction in manual labor and an exponential improvement in reliability and results. These solutions tackle the complex task of analysing vast amounts of data, save valuable time and provide better information, providing significant operational benefits.

Revenue Management Culture

Hotels with automated RM benefit from a consistent deployment of RM practices from person-to-person, hotel-to-hotel and across large chains. Organisations that invest in building a RM culture around a highly sophisticated and integrated tool jeopardise both benefits and culture if they discontinue using that tool for any period of time.

Some of the most respected hotel companies in the world, such as Hilton International, work hand-in-hand with solution providers to "..develop and enhance ..integrated revenue systems, ensuring that Yield underpins our strategy." The benefits of maintaining a consistent revenue management culture are tangible in the superior RevPAR and competitive set performance of hotels with automated RM solutions.

Group demand

In today's market, more pressure is put on properties to reduce rates and renegotiate group contracts. Automated solutions enable hotels to evaluate potential business that might be displaced by accepting a particular group, evaluating days prior to arrival and after departure. They provide comprehensive scenario evaluation and rapid response to group inquiries. Through automated solutions, properties now have access to tools that quantify the impact of making these types of strategic changes on group business, enabling them to evaluate and accept the right mix of groups versus transient business.

Maximising contract revenue

Contract business builds a solid base business for hotels and may account for a significant amount of a hotel's business. A revolutionary new RM tool for contract evaluation provides properties with the ability to negotiate more profitable contracts. Automated solutions provide tools to objectively measure the financial impact of potential contracts and provides management with the ability to make more informed decisions about rates and access (yieldable, semi-yieldable, non-yieldable).

Despite current market conditions, hotels are entering the important contract season and this capability is invaluable in maintaining inventory flexibility and maximising revenue from contract business.

Managing market resurgence

Having an automated RM system installed and operating as the market revives is essential. Hotels worldwide will experience subtle increases in group inquiries, conversion rates and occupancy that automated systems are designed to detect. Each of these events represents critical revenue maximising opportunities. Hotel properties with automated RM systems installed and operating will have competitive advantages in both short and long-term performance.

In today's market, every opportunity to maximise revenue is critical to the success and longevity of hotel properties. As hotels worldwide anticipate recovery and the return of business, having the appropriate solutions in place is not only practical, it's imperative. Automated RM solutions provide strategic competitive advantages and quantifiable benefits.

9

Hospitality Partnerships

Public sector support for hospitality development has been episodic and erratic in the United States and elsewhere in the world as economic development policies have shifted. When government has commonly stepped in, support has focused on the development of key hotel properties deemed essential to stimulate business travel and tourism, and create new jobs. Formal public/private alliances in these cases have often opened the door to lower-cost financing of hotel development, as well as a host of other incentives to stimulate private investment.

Public entities have at their disposal a wide array of programmes and financial vehicles that can assist in making a hotel project feasible and thus contribute to an area's overall economic well-being. The potential to access lower-cost financing, tap redevelopment incentives, structure favorable land lease terms, secure site improvements and other alternatives should not be overlooked by hotel developers when development projects have a clear link to public interests.

Public financing of private hotel investment is not new in the United States. The Small Business Administration (SBA), for example, has financed the development of smaller hotels since the mid 1950s. In the past four years, loans provided by the SBA for hotels were approximately three percent of total SBA loans, and the average size was $560,000.

Most commonly, however, public financing and other incentives to promote hospitality investment in the United States have arisen at the local level in development of convention headquarters hotels, which are essential to the success of these large meeting and trade show facilities. Conventions are big business in the United States with more than 800,000 national meetings held annually, much of that market dominated by corporate bookings. Collectively, these conventions attracted some 55 million attendees in 1993.

The more than 500 public and private convention and meeting centers in the United States, in fact, typically form a linchpin in the economic development strategies of local and regional governments. Convention center development and expansion have been components of local economic development strategies since the mid-1980s and continue to rise. Three new centers opened in the last 18 months at locations in Charlotte, North Carolina; Mobile, Alabama; and outside Washington, D.C. And a 1994 Tradeshow Week survey indicated that more than 60 percent of U.S. convention centers were considering expansion — versus only 31 percent in 1993. Planned expansions of exhibition space in convention centers are expected to generate 58.8 million square feet as of 1994, climbing to 64 million by 1999.

The interdependent economics of convention centers and the hotels that serve them create opportunities for public/private partnerships of benefit to government entities and private investors. The evolution of public/private partnerships to support development of convention headquarters hotels, as a result, offer an excellent foundation for examining how public sector financing and other incentives can support private hotel investment.

Most cities require a convention headquarters hotel to market their convention center successfully. Yet many mid- to upper-tier cities often lack sufficient hotel inventory that can be specifically committed to this purpose. Conversely, room nights generated from a convention center are often insufficient to exclusively support a convention headquarters hotel serving the meetings and trade shows so important to local economies. Further complicating the problem, convention headquarters hotels often incur higher than typical development costs due to the amount and quality of public areas required. The result — a need for public/private partnerships to support the economic feasibility of a convention headquarters hotel. This hotel, in turn, will support the public investment made in a convention center, as well as generating other local economic benefits.

These public/private partnerships have therefore become increasingly critical as convention center facilities have proliferated in the United States. They also evidence the range of options available to the public sector to support private hotel development. While these types of incentives most often may be used to support convention hotels, they may also be important tools for other types of hotel projects in which there is a strong relationship between public interests and private investment.

Economics of Convention-oriented Hotel

Nearly 65 percent of U.S. convention centers are owned by cities, counties, states or other types of government authorities. Major convention cities, such as New York or Las Vegas, generally have had sufficient hotel supply in appropriate locations to support the needs generated by meeting and trade show participants. For many other municipalities, however, new hotel development can be critical to competing for the middle-to upper-tier convention market. Convention facilities in these cities may be located in areas peripheral to hotel concentrations. In addition, existing hotel operators are often reluctant to commit the room inventory required to serve convention delegates — typically offered in package deals at lower room rates — while simultaneously reducing rooms available to serve guests that make up their core business.

The basic economics in hotel development and operations pose additional challenges. Convention-oriented hotels are typically 10 to 20 percent more expensive to develop than a comparable size, group-oriented hotel. At the same time, room rates for a convention hotel's core market segment may run 20 to 30 percent below comparable business hotels due to discount package deals negotiated for delegates as part of convention attendance.

To remain successful, a convention center must attract annual national bookings in the range of 25 to 30 events that have a minimum of 2,500 participants each. These bookings, however, on average support occupancies of only 30 to 35 percent in terms of total room nights. As a result of these factors, convention center hotel properties must either achieve higher average occupancies, develop other sources of business or realise higher room rates attributable to non-convention guests to succeed.

Convention hotels can often attract alternative sources of revenue, including sponsoring convention and meeting trade separate from a convention center. Sources of business may include smaller group business, commercial activity, and wholesale and tour operator business. Nevertheless, the hotel is in most cases fundamentally dependent on the convention center for its core business. To entice new development, local government entities must often work jointly with hotel developers to overcome the obstacles that tend to make these hotels more costly to develop and less profitable to operate.

Initiatives prior to the 1986 Tax Reform Act pointed the way to creative forms of public/private partnerships serving the interests of convention centers and their headquarters hotels. The City of Miami, for example, provided an array of incentives to attract hotel development in support of the James I. Knight Center. The city acquired land, provided a 45-year lease with attractive terms and furnished off-site improvements, as well as site utilities. The hotel additionally was awarded the food & beverage concession for the convention center, and real estate property taxes were abated during construction.

The incentives provided by the City of Toledo at Seagate Center is another case in point. A $7.4 million Urban Development Action Grant was loaned to the developer through the Convention Bureau at attractive rates and terms. Tax increment financing was used to support public improvements, while real estate taxes were abated. In addition, the hotel was supplied with convention center-owned parking at prevailing market rates.

More recent public/private partnership successes include the Westin Hotel venture in Providence, Rhode Island, which involved a $290 million bond issue, that covered the convention center, hotel and parking. A Sheraton Hotel at the Jefferson Center in Birmingham, Alabama, involved a $148 million low-interest bond offering, guaranteed by JCA and supported by city and county occupational taxes.

Not all public/private partnerships come together, despite concerted efforts on the part of both private developers and public entities. In Tampa, studies indicated a strong need for a convention hotel to support the city's new convention center. A city commission approved a proposed 900-room Marriott hotel, estimated to cost more than $140 million or more, and to be owned by a private 'not for profit' corporation. A special task force spent six months analysing two options and is presently formulating recommendations.

The dilemma faced in Los Angeles also is a case in point. A major expansion of the Los Angeles Convention Center was completed late last year, increasing total meeting space to more than 600,000 square feet. Historically, however, the center has hosted only about 20 conventions annually, and competition from other Western cities — including San Francisco, San Diego, Anaheim, Long Beach, Seattle, Portland and Las Vegas — has become more intense. The Los Angeles

Convention and Visitors Bureau has contended that a convention hotel within walking distance is required to make the city more competitive for attracting large conventions. Yet the downtown Los Angeles hotel market has been weak since the onset of the recession early in this decade, a condition which has been further exacerbated by the Los Angeles riots in 1992 and the Northridge earthquake last year.

Downtown's primary convention hotels, all located within seven blocks of the convention center, collectively posted occupancies in the mid-50 percent range last year (up more than six occupancy points from one of the worst years in recorded history) with projected occupancies edging toward 60 percent this year. Thus far, it has been concluded that a major new convention hotel is not economically feasible, even with generous public incentives.

Public and Private Contributions

These initiatives demonstrate the range of strategies available to the private sector to attract private hotel investment — as well as the pitfalls that can create obstacles. At their best, these partnerships make it possible to reduce hotel development costs, set the stage for more profitable hotel operations, and allow a government jurisdiction to safeguard public investment and achieve local economic development goals.

Generally, public contributions that can drive development of a hotel may include land at favorable lease terms, off-street parking facilities, construction/use rights of public space and marketing support. Hotel developers may also be granted the convention center's food and beverage service concession. This ancillary revenue can be an important step to offset the lower room rates often associated with delegate business. Among the contributions made by the hotel developer are equity funding, the track record of team members, a superior product development plan, and strong management and marketing.

In addition, the public and private entities must have controls in place to ensure that relationship objectives are maintained. A convention headquarters hotel, for example, must commit room nights to the convention center, even at the cost of displacing higher rated business. Conversely, the convention center must book events, which generate room nights, perhaps foregoing higher revenue-generating consumer shows that tend to be oriented to a local audience.

A range of successful private/public techniques are available to further these partnerships:

Site Control

Land values in urban or resort environments are generally very high with these costs typically representing a significant component of hotel development. Government participation is often essential, either by writing down the market value of a property or purchasing a property to lease to a hotel owner on a long-term basis at an economic cost.

Miami Beach's experience is instructive. The city in 1992 expanded its existing convention center located near City Hall, a location remote from Miami Beach's highly developed existing hotels. No new major hotels have been developed in 27 years. Studies commissioned by the city addressed several pivotal issues. It was determined that none of the existing hotels — clustered primarily at some distance along the coastline— would or could continuously sell room nights to major national conventions that desire to book the city's convention center. Additionally, major hotel developers would be unlikely to develop a new hotel away from the beach area without significant incentives. Arthur Andersen was asked to advise the city on incentive parameters required to entice developers and financial institutions in the development and financing of the 800-room hotel. Among the most important of the incentives was site control.

Arthur Andersen advisors concluded that the city's purchase of the site adjacent or proximate to the convention center was essential. It was further determined that the hotel site should have ocean-front exposure. After analysis of three potential locations, the city purchased an ocean-front site at a cost of $24 million. The site is five blocks from the city's convention center.

Low-cost Financing

In the past five years, new full-service hotels have been extremely difficult to finance. Convention hotels, furthermore, are generally regarded as being of even higher risk — a result of the uncertainty related to occupancies and above-average development costs. As a result, public financing can be the key element in making a convention center hotel feasible.

Again, a number of options are available to the public sector. While tax- exempt public bond issues are subject to 'private purpose' limitations, there are techniques which can blend in public funding to privately owned and operated hotel ventures. These include financing and leasing back the 'public' areas of a hotel (or a parking, etc.) facility. Public revenues from hotel taxes or real property taxes may be designated for the facility through non-tax exempt issues. In addition, cities, counties and other government entities may offer certain operating guarantees, such as payment of debt service, for a specified period of time.

In some cases cities have made equity investments in convention hotels. The municipality may become the junior equity partner in the hotel with 'first-in' risk capital, and 'last-out' return. In a broad policy sense, the city's rate of return is potentially greatly enhanced by an improved local economy, higher visitation and associated tax revenues.

Bond financing, and public ownership of the asset, for example, is a cornerstone of the financing structure for a new convention center hotel at McCormick Place, the final phase of its exposition center. The Metropolitan Pier and Exposition Authority, which controls McCormick Place, announced in March of this year that it plans to raise $110 million through a bond issue for the development of a new hotel adjacent to the center. The Authority will own the hotel, which is to have a minimum of 400 rooms and likely more. A third party will be selected to operate the property.

Other Public Incentives

Local governments also have incentive options that will have significant impact on the economies of building a convention headquarters hotel. These include incorporating public spaces and amenities, such as joint parking or meeting facilities to reduce the overall cost of the convention hotel. Municipalities may also provide property tax abatements, as well as redevelopment zone benefits such as expedited permitting and access to other public funding sources.

Structuring the Deal

From a development and operational standpoint, there are a number of challenges facing hotel companies as they consider convention headquarters hotels. In addition, many deals have failed because a city has insufficient resources to close a transaction, or lacks an understanding of the resources it can bring to bear in support of these developments. What is fundamentally at stake is shifting a portion of the risk from the developer to public entities, since the public jurisdiction stands to benefit economically if the hotel is a success.

More than a standard Request for Proposal (RFP) to attract a quality developer is often needed. The public sector must understand what types of incentives it has available to drive a project — and the best way to frame the RFP process. And it will clearly require specialised expertise to ensure that financial incentive structures make the most of available opportunities and that the expectations are realistic.

In setting parameters for competitive bidding on these projects, municipalities or other public jurisdictions need to be specific about certain factors, such as the hotel size, design, quality of facilities and amenities, and management. But rather than defining the competition in a rigid envelope, it is more important to ensure that respondents customise a proposal that meets the city's criteria and defined needs, and includes financial structures crafted to match the public resources available. Clearly defined procedures for evaluation of proposals are also crucial.

Hotel development can generate a significant stream of economic benefits for a community including support for a tourism industry, job creation and an expanded tax base. Public incentives to support private hotel investment, as a result, can become a decisive component required to assure that public economic development goals are achieved.

Partnership of Sales and Technology

The hospitality industry has used innovation and imagination to manipulate and maximise tech applications for everything from revenue management to customer relationship management. Why then have we not given more thought to the creative uses of technology in the hotel sales process?

One answer is that while we have provided upgraded tech access to our guests, the sales department and administrative offices usually get hand-me-down hardware and sometimes are not even included in the high-speed Internet equation. Current web sites are often like the old cover letters that sales people used to use for every inquiry and follow-up. Those were the letters that "feature spewed" by having a list of every conceivable feature in bullet points regardless of the type of client that it was addressed to. The following are a few of the ways that hotel sales can use these tech tools to sell customers on the benefits of the hotel not just tell them about its features:

Virtual Tours

Virtual tours are great tools. As busy as most people are today, it is often difficult to get potential customers even from the same city to a hotel for a site inspection. However, rather than have the customer log onto the web site or take the virtual tour alone, why not establish a telephone appointment so that the client and the sales person can walk through the site while on the phone together? This allows the sales person to point out the features of the hotel that are true benefits to this customer and to sell the hotel's services. The sales person should prepare for this site presentation in the same way that they would for a "live" site inspection. The good news is that with a virtual tour, you don't have to pre-inspect the rooms and it usually doesn't cost you lunch.

In developing virtual tours on the web site, keep in mind that the average attention span of most people is relatively short. Pick the most representative digital photography for inclusion but limit your selections to those that will have the broadest appeal. Granted it was a large hotel but when you have seen one boardroom, you've pretty much seen them all.

Digital Photography

The "bank" of photography was the same as those used to build the web site. However, there were also some that were not used on the site. Most of the phone calls were from potential customers who had visited the site but had questions or concerns or simply wanted to speak to a live human versus making their reservations on-line.

Photography more often "sells" when it includes people using a feature of the hotel. For example, rather than simply having a photograph of the children's camp or playground, photos of children playing and having fun using these facilities sell the concept rather than just telling that the facility is there. Recall those stock photos of a hotel restaurant where people are sitting at the table staring at each other but not actually eating or drinking or appearing to have fun. The people in those photos were like the furniture.

The sales staff can use this photography in much the same way. Even if a planner has come for a "live" site, they often forget certain features. Many of them are coming to look at many hotels on the same trip. Depending upon the number of hotels that they tour, their memory will often place the bathroom of one hotel in another hotel's guest room. An emailed photo will refresh their memory or speak to question or concern. It can be a powerful tool to reinforce their initial impression and overcome a potential objection. For other groups, it can also provide an image of a benefit that a client requires in one situation that they didn't require in a previous meeting.

Photography of your destination and area attractions can assist you in making the sale and promoting off-site activities. This is more powerful than simply referring them to the local tourist organisation's web site where they will also be exposed to other properties and perhaps rates.

Email Postcards

Sales people are always looking for creative ways to stay in touch with accounts. Email postcards can fill this requirement if kept fresh and not overused. Postcards, on the other hand, receive a glance prior to being thrown away. You at least have a shot at gaining the recipients attention. Unsolicited attachments to emails are like mailings in envelopes. Busy people trying to manage their Inboxes most often delete them prior to opening. In addition, people are loath to open attachments that they are not expecting due to viruses.

An email postcard opens automatically. The visual appears in the recipients Inbox and is at least glanced at prior to deleting. This is an opportunity to gain the recipient's attention. Be very careful about not using this medium in a manner that could be considered "spam" —

it should not be blasted to anyone who hasn't given "permission" to receive information about your hotel.

Let's differentiate between email "blasts" and approaching a potential new client. Email blasts to large number of recipients are extremely useful in informing past and potential customers about new developments or promotions at a property to those who have indicated a desire to receive them. An email postcard can be a way to approach a prospect when telephone contact has failed as it does frequently. This is a tailored communication to one person versus a mass communication to many.

These are not to be used for email "blasts" but for customised communication to prospects and clients, especially when phone calls and regular emails get lost in the "chatter" of hotel solicitations. These postcards can set you apart from your competitors. It's a tough market out there. Sales people need creative tools to push the process forward.

Those who are able to relate to their clients in a technologically sophisticated way exemplify that the property and the sales staff are prepared to offer their clients the services required in a high-speed environment. Sales is the engine that drives revenue. Investing in tech tools and training sales people to use them enables them to sell in such an environment. By ensuring that they have access to these tools, the property's exposure is enhanced.

The Partnership Not the Disconnect

Groups and conventions are booming – a significant increase over previous years. Competition is stiff and the window to submit proposals is shortening. Evaluating the quality of a group booking for all profit centers is critical. For those of you with sophisticated revenue management systems this process is not as difficult as for some hotels who are doing revenue management the 'old fashioned' way and there are more of those than you might think – even among large group houses and companies! However, even some sophisticated revenue management systems struggle with the integration and analysis of the value of catering revenue and it's impact on the overall revenue management strategy.

Sales managers now not only have to sell the client or meeting planner but also sell the revenue manager on the 'worthiness' of a piece of business. This has always been the case to some extent but it is more critical than ever that sales understands the revenue management strategy and process.

Below are a few considerations for sales managers to evaluate a group if you don't have a sophisticated revenue management system to work with. In making a case for a specific group whose rate may fall at or below the RM parameters but has a significant impact on the other profit centers requires research and diplomacy. It is also a valuable process when you want to make a case for an 'exception' for a group.

— *Evaluate Past Revenue History of the Property.* Pull the revenue history for all profit centers, rooms, catering, F&B outlets, spa, etc., for the past two years. Were there groups in house that influenced this revenue and, if so, what was the revenue profile of the past group in terms of room rate, etc.? How does the current group's revenue contribution compare to previous groups? You will also need to source the rest of the sales department in relation to group bids others may be working on for the same dates and which may have better overall revenue potential for the hotel.

— *Understand the Revenue Goals of Each Profit Center.* Here is where diplomacy plays a major role. Each profit center may become an ally if you know how this group is going to make a significant contribution to their revenue goals for the period. Helping other departments get what they want is a great way to get what you want.

— *Obtain the Group's Past History.* Most companies and organisations know exactly what they spent on this meeting or similar ones in the past in terms of rooms, F&B, catering, etc. If the history varies significantly from what they have told you they anticipate, it should set off a 'red flag' – ask them why they believe this group or meeting will be different from past ones.

— *Qualify for Future Potential.* This requires that you completely qualify the account for future business prior to booking this group. Be careful – it's like the contractor who went to purchase 5 refrigerators for a development he was building but told the salesman he needed five hundred. The salesman put together his best deal. The contractor took only the five and never went back for the other 495. We've all been on the short end of this tactic at one time or the other. If they are asking for concessions on this group, tie it to a contract on a future group – have them sign both contracts.

— *Be Prepared to Walk Away.* This is a tough one. Good sales people love to book business and then there is the question of the quota and/or bonus for the period. The faster you walk away from a piece of business that is not aligned with the hotel's revenue management strategy the faster you can move on to other prospects. In addition, if the bonus or incentive system is not aligned with the revenue management strategy, and many are not, it is a huge source of contention and the source of the 'disconnect' between sales and revenue management, therefore making the sales person even more reluctant to walk away.

The incentive system should reward revenue booked during opportunity periods at a higher value than business booked in peak season. It doesn't take a great deal of talent to sell business in periods of high demand and, if the bonus is based on rooms not revenue, that business may be sold at a lower than optimal rate and still be rewarded.

Broadway Hospitality

The Texas-based hotel management firm currently operates 20 hotels in six states. Its properties include some of the most easily recognisable brand names in the industry such as Holiday Inns, Wyndham Hotels, and Marriott Hotels. The Sales and Revenue Team at Broadway Hospitality are dedicated to maximising market share by anticipating changes in the marketplace, and reacting quickly to develop new and innovative strategies to meet those changes.

Broadway Hospitality believes that growth depends upon driving financial results in its hotels. The Knowland Group shares this philosophy. The firm works to provide new products that adapt to ever-changing needs. The management at Knowland recognises that success means being in front of the pack.

Habits of Sales People

There are sales people who come to the industry with no previous experience in hotels and are highly successful – outperforming their colleagues who may have been in hotel sales for many years. Usually but not always these are people who have come from commission sales of some sort. It is not necessarily the fact that other industries have better training programmes (although many industries do a better and far more consistent job than much of the hotel industry), it is not just the sense of urgency that comes with having to create an income every month, it also has to do with the habits that they must develop in order to successfully pay the mortgage and eat.

— *Daily Disciplines — Eating the Elephant One Bite at a Time.* Successful sales people take their goals, revenue, prospecting, calls etc. and break them down into monthly, weekly, daily activities. They have a good idea of their call to closing ratio, that is, how many calls, telephone or e-contacts, they need to make to close a contract. They know how many prospects they need to locate in a day and a week to meet their prospecting goals. They practice 'daily disciplines' every day.

— *Prioritise Activities.* Not all activities, calls, traces, etc, are created equal. Prioritised sales people call on those prospects most likely to produce revenue before they do the trace calls to say 'hello' to existing accounts – they prioritise their calls. They will cancel the Chamber of Commerce lunch if a prospective client wants to see them. They make time to prospect and pre-approach qualify prospects on the Internet AND they do that in non-prime sales time.

— *Think Revenue not Just Rooms.* The successful sales person pays attention to the property's revenue management strategy and understands that the name of the game is revenue – not rooms. The revenue management strategy informs their prospecting activities. For example, in the SMERF market, the group of wine enthusiasts is more likely to pay the rate than the local scrap bookers club.

— *Whales and Tunas.* Successful sales people know that they need a mix of both large and small groups and accounts to meet their revenue goals and to balance out the group calendar. Some sales people only want to pursue the big 'glamour' accounts. The problem with that is it takes much longer to land them than the smaller, less flashy, tunas. If the whale doesn't close within the timeframe of the sales persons goals, the sales person may not be there when the whale account eventually signs the contract.

— *'Intra-preneurs'*. Successful sales people treat their market or their territory like a business – their business. They function as intraprenuers within the organisation. That makes them think creative and allows them to think out of the box in addressing issues within the organisations on their client's behalf.

— *Personal (Brutally Honest) SWOT Analysis.* Successful sales people evaluate their strengths in order to leverage it in to more business and maybe even a better position for themselves –don't forget the WIIFM factor! They are also honest about the areas where they could use some training and/or support and actively ask for it or seek out opportunities to get the training they need. They seek out opportunities in their market area and never underestimate the potential threats of competitors.

— *Sense of Urgency.* Successful sales people have a sense of urgency about working their plan because they know that if they fall too far behind it will be very difficult to catch up. They stay late when they have to and ask to leave early when they are caught up. Their sense of urgency is focused and directed not just a sense of urgency about activity, any activity. They choose their association memberships and functions carefully so that they only participate in those likely to be a source of business.

Bibliography

Busby, G., "The changing role of staff development for travel and tourism lecturers", *Journal of the National Association for Staff Development in Further and Higher Education*, 33, 1995.

Cooper, C., "An analysis of the relationship between industry and education in travel and tourism", *Teoros International*, 1(1), 1993.

Chen, K. and Groves, D., "The importance of examining philosophical relationships between tourism and hospitality curricula", *International Journal of Contemporary Hospitality Management*, 1999.

Daurer, C., "Qualification in tourism - a challenge for education and training", *Tourism and Hospitality Management*, 2001.

Ellias, S., "The future of tourism and hospitality management courses", *Tourism Management*, 1992.

Evans, J., "Tourism graduates: a case of over production?", *Tourism Management*, 1993.

Fletcher, J. and Latham, J., "International tourism training", *Tourism Management*, 1989.

Formica, S., "European hospitality and tourism education: differences with the American model and future trends", *International Journal of Hospitality Management*, 1996.

Gee, C., "Professionalisation and travel industry education", *The Journal of Hospitality Education*, 4(2), 1980.

Lavery, P., "Education and training in tourism, in S. Witt & L. Moutinho", *Tourism Marketing and Management Handbook*, New York, Prentice Hall (119-122), 1989.

Leiper, N., "Tourism systems: An interdisciplinary perspective", *Occasional Paper* 2, Palmerston, Massey University, 1990.

Leslie, D, "Higher education for hospitality and tourism: a European destination", *International Journal of Hospitality Management*, 12(1), pp. 101-107, 1993.

Pendleton, Tom, "Young People and Bicycle Touring", Velo City '01 Conference, Edinburgh, Glasgow, September 2001.

Pizam, Abraham & Mansfield, Yoel, "Consumer Behavior in Travel and Tourism", The Haworth Hospitality Press, Binghampton, New York, 1999.

Prideaux, B., "The role of the transport system in destination development", (Elsevier) *Journal of Tourism Management* 21 (1), December, 1999.

Index